Digital Media, Denunciation and Shaming

This book offers a common set of concepts to help make sense of online shaming practices, accounting for instances of discrimination and injury that morally divide readers and at times risk unjust and disproportionate harm to those under scrutiny.

Digital media denunciation has become a primary form of expression and entertainment across media environments, with new socially desirable forms of accountability under movements such as #MeToo and #BlackLivesMatter addressing longstanding forms of systematic and interpersonal abuse. Building on recent scholarship on shaming, surveillance and denunciation in fixed contexts, this study generates a cross-contextual and multi-actor account of practices like 'cancel culture,' 'doxing' and 'status degradation ceremonies.' It addresses instances of moral ambivalence by discussing how digital shaming becomes normalised and embedded across socio-cultural and institutional settings. The authors establish key actors and practices in online denunciations of individuals in a range of cases and contexts, including responses to COVID-19, political polarisation, and social justice movements, as well as more local and quotidian circumstances. They draw from empirical data including interviews with nearly 100 individuals targeted by mediated shaming and/or involved in these practices, as well as ethnographic observations of digital vigilantism and discourse analysis of press coverage and online comments relating to online shaming. Diverse applications and contexts, including China, the UK, Russia and Central Asia, are considered, advancing an ambivalent understanding of media and denunciation that reconciles progressive and regressive practices, as well as celebratory and critical accounts of these practices.

This book is recommended reading for advanced students and researchers of online visibility and harm across media studies, cultural studies and sociology.

Daniel Trottier is Associate Professor of Global Digital Media in the Department of Media and Communication, Erasmus Universiteit Rotterdam, the Netherlands.

Qian Huang is Assistant Professor in the Centre for Media and Journalism Studies, University of Groningen, the Netherlands.

Rashid Gabdulhakov is Assistant Professor in the Centre for Media and Journalism Studies, University of Groningen, the Netherlands.

Routledge Focus on Communication and Society

Series Editor: James Curran

Routledge Focus on Communication and Society offers both established and early-career academics the flexibility to publish cutting-edge analysis on topical issues, research on new media or in-depth case studies within the broad field of media, communication and cultural studies. Its main concerns are whether the media empower or fail to empower popular forces in society; media organisations and public policy; and the political and social consequences of the media.

Bad News from Venezuela
Alan MacLeod

Reporting China on the Rise
Yuan Zeng

Alternative Right-Wing Media
Kristoffer Holt

Disinformation and Manipulation in Digital Media
Information Pathologies
Eileen Culloty and Jane Suiter

Social Media and Hate
Shakuntala Banaji and Ramnath Bhat

The Construction of News in a Polarised State
Lessons in Maltese Advocacy Journalism
Adrian Hillman

News Media and the Financial Crisis
How Elite Journalism Undermined the Case for a Paradigm Shift
Adam Cox

Digital Media, Denunciation and Shaming
The Court of Public Opinion
Daniel Trottier, Qian Huang and Rashid Gabdulhakov

For more information about this series, please visit: https://www.routledge.com/Routledge-Focus-on-Communication-and-Society/book-series/00RFCS

Digital Media, Denunciation and Shaming

The Court of Public Opinion

Daniel Trottier, Qian Huang and Rashid Gabdulhakov

First published 2025
by Routledge
4 Park Square, Milton Park, Abingdon, Oxon OX14 4RN

and by Routledge
605 Third Avenue, New York, NY 10158

Routledge is an imprint of the Taylor & Francis Group, an informa business

British Library Cataloguing-in-Publication Data
A catalogue record for this book is available from the British Library

Library of Congress Cataloging-in-Publication Data
Names: Trottier, Daniel, author. | Huang, Qian, author. |
Gabdulhakov, Rashid, author.
Title: Digital media, denunciation and shaming: the court of public
opinion / Daniel Trottier, Qian Huang and Rashid Gabdulhakov.
Description: Abingdon, Oxon; New York, NY: Routledge, 2025. |
Series: Routledge focus on communication and society |
Includes bibliographical references and index.
Identifiers: LCCN 2024015514 (print) | LCCN 2024015515 (ebook) |
Subjects: LCSH: Public opinion. | Internet–Social aspects. | Shame. |
Cancel culture.
Classification: LCC HM1236 .T76 2025 (print) | LCC HM1236 (ebook) |
DDC 302.23/1–dc23/eng/20240521
LC record available at https://lccn.loc.gov/2024015514
LC ebook record available at https://lccn.loc.gov/2024015515

ISBN: 9781032602721 (hbk)
ISBN: 9781032602738 (pbk)
ISBN: 9781003453017 (ebk)

DOI: 10.4324/9781003453017

Typeset in Times New Roman

by Deanta Global Publishing Services, Chennai, India

This research was funded by the Dutch Research Council (NWO), project number 276-45-004 and file number 36.201.097.

Contents

1 Introducing the court of public opinion

From slacktivism to stay-at-home vigilantism

COVID-19 had a lasting impact on social relations. This is obvious to anybody who had an argument with their family about lockdowns or vaccines. In addition to new public health measures, new social norms were quickly implemented. People expected others to wear masks in public, maintain physical distance and limit unnecessary social contact. As a consequence, we witnessed emerging forms of actionable behaviour. In the early stages of the pandemic, hoarding toilet paper and unnecessary travel sparked public ire. More prominent figures also became targets following revelations of insider trading linked to the crisis, as well as for appearing to flout public health restrictions.

The term 'covidiot' has entered public discourse as a category of target who violates pandemic-related rules and norms.[1] While many of these offences have provoked outrage previously, the unexpected, uncertain and upsetting conditions of the pandemic sharpened public sentiment against those caught breaking these rules. In the case of a prominent influencer who used personal connections to get tested, a US tabloid dubbed her a "covidiot" in the title of their writeup.[2] This is one way the press actively contribute to public denunciation, while attributing this outrage to a rabid online mob. For the influencer deemed a covidiot, negative outcomes were framed in terms of damage to her personal brand, a commoditised extension of her personal reputation. Because of the public denunciation against her, any business endeavour that makes use of her public status is now less viable. Social media users also used the term covidiot to denounce a celebrity doctor accused of spreading misinformation.[3] On Twitter,[4] one of the top comments refers to cancel culture as "*exactly* the right response." By endorsing cancel culture, this poster asserts that medical professionals have no place in the public eye if they abuse their credentials to spread misinformation. They should be excluded from public and professional networks, while their reputation is openly tarnished as a warning against other potential wrongdoers.

Also at the start of the pandemic, American right-wing media figure Charlie Kirk called upon his followers to report on ideological opponents employed in education.[5] Because all in-class teaching suddenly migrated

DOI: 10.4324/9781003453017-1

online, it became easier to scrutinise. In combating what he frames as left-wing indoctrination of students, Kirk's call for denunciations marks a shift from targeting celebrities to targeting a broader category of labourer, many of whom working under precarious conditions. This is a proactive strategy, as his Twitter followers are urged to seek out, capture and disseminate evidence of political advocacy among teachers. This scrutiny can easily creep into other contexts. When targeting someone on the internet, it is easy to not only monitor their professional content, but also any other personal details online. A teacher's Twitter account may bridge their professional and personal lives by making both visible to a wider public.

The practice of experiencing one's social world and judging neighbours through digital platforms is a pressing concern (Andrejevic, 2007). These issues became even more troubling when global lockdowns led to even more interactions taking place through screens. Researchers and users need to reflect on the media practices that have become routinised through these digital windows to the world. There are many ways that individuals seek social change online. Some efforts like online petitions have been dismissed as slacktivism, as they seemingly fail to mobilise a broader public response and social outcome. Critics disregard online mobilisation as a feel-good spectacle, with little to no material impact.[6] Yet tangible change is possible: reporting on peers for the purposes of denouncing them as well as bringing symbolic and material harm, including harassment (Marwick, 2021). People can make a target visible in order to hold them accountable. While this seems like a user-led practice, those users have no control over the media frenzy that follows. Someone who launches a denunciation may have an objective in mind. They can take the first step in uploading evidence of a misdeed. The consequences that follow will be determined by a complex global media landscape. This leads to three concerns. First, a lack of proportionality: the risk that public punishment exceeds a reasonable idea of retribution and justice. People routinely receive death threats for minor transgressions, including challenging someone's opinion on Twitter. Second, there is often no feasible route towards resolution and reintegration of the target. Online apologies are often met with derision, and those targeted may bear their stigma indefinitely. Third, from individual offences, stigma and prejudice are broadly applied to communities that the target seemingly represents, whether based on ethnicity, nationality, gender, sexual orientation, class or religion. Public shaming of norm violations can serve as grounds for public attacks on vulnerable communities deemed responsible (cf. Cai & Tolan, 2020).

Concerns of slacktivism are valid, as deliberate and desirable social change is not always feasible through the internet. What audiences encounter instead are attempts to damage someone's public image and employability. This occurs through mediated scrutiny, denunciation and shaming. Mediated scrutiny is a ubiquitous practice that can be performed by any social actor to watch over the actions and utterances of any public-facing individual.

Mediated denunciation is performed by media actors like content creators, as an open announcement of someone's misdeeds. Whereas denunciation is conventionally understood as communicated to a state, church or other authority (Bergemann, 2017), individuals may now bypass these authorities in reporting a target to a mediated audience. And while denunciation is an open announcement of someone's misdeeds by a particular actor or set of actors, shaming is a crowdsourced moral degradation that may be accompanied by other forms of abuse (Trottier, 2018a). The actions taken on by the bulk of participants resemble the minimal effort of slacktivism: viewing content, clicking 'like,' sharing the content and posting comments. So-called online shitstorms are made up of these practices, as well as capturing footage or screenshots, and more drastic measures like 'swatting,' or summoning a police response against a target under false pretences (Enzweiler, 2014). The image of digital media users as slackers is incomplete. So-called slacktivism can effect change, both regressive and progressive though never proportionate. We may instead use terms like vigilantes to describe these actors (cf. Trottier, 2017). This term signals users' independence from the state and media organisations like the press. Yet user-led denunciations are in fact entangled across media platforms that also host employers, advertisers and public authorities.

Scrutiny, denunciation and shaming

Digital media users denounce and shame others in response to perceived moral and legal offences. This operates through a collective and publicly visible lowering of a person's perceived social value. While shaming is celebrated in some cases of longstanding abuse such as #MeToo, it can also be disproportionate in response and draw criticism from diverse actors. The opening cases are best understood as a set of digitally mediated practices that include denunciation as well as unwanted attention and engagement. These practices are a consequence of contemporary mediated visibility, as the people implicated are public-facing due to a range of everyday media practices at the workplace and in personal settings. These events matter because they are highly visible affirmations about the targeted person's reputation – their social worth in the eyes of their peers. Scrutinising and denouncing others enables a kind of court of public opinion based on how individuals may form and utilise judgements about others. We propose the term 'court of public opinion' to identify the process of scrutiny, denunciation and shaming. Yet we acknowledge and engage below with other suitable terms used to describe these processes, including social sanction, accountability and cancel culture, as well as doxing,[7] digital vigilantism and online shitstorms in more ramped-up cases.

This court of public opinion is routinised and embedded in everyday life. Canadian podcaster Noreta Leto offers a concise account of this term in stating the "court of public opinion is a thing that exists because we ask people what they think about people all the time."[8] Opinion-seeking from trusted peers is a fundamental social process, to the extent that people may neglect to recognise it as a process. It may easily go unnamed and unnoticed, until these opinions harm one's standing. The court's status as "a thing that exists" is uncertain and contested. We may not recognise these practices because they are mundane and ubiquitous, for instance when asking a friend whether a potential roommate or mechanic is trustworthy. These courts may exist as private and protected social networks, or as more overt – yet exclusionary – platforms. They may be restricted to an institutional setting like a workplace, yet the contemporary use of digital media pushes these courts to be open and visible, transcending cultural and contextual boundaries.

Online scrutiny is often also obscured from public view when taking on systemic and categorical forms of abuse. The so-called whisper network in various professional communities serves to mitigate longstanding patterns of gendered violence (Tuerkheimer, 2019). And accountability practices like cancel culture and callouts emerge from Black and other marginalised counterpublics (Clark, 2020). Yet despite progressive applications, online shaming often reflects and extends upon offline inequalities, as well as political and ideological pursuits. Individuals and groups marginalised in terms of gender, race and sexuality are vulnerable to the act of online shaming and the subsequent outcomes that may lead to job loss, resentment and prolonged offline persecution. The use of social media to expose those in power sometimes backfires and harms the accusers, as in the case of young women in China denouncing powerful men for sexual misconduct, who themselves became targets of public denunciation (Yin & Sun, 2021).

The court of public opinion is ubiquitous. It is part of everyday social and cultural experience. Scrutiny and denunciation of other individuals as basic social practices are now amplified and archived through digital media. As a result of being embedded in contemporary digital media cultures, the court of public opinion is manifest almost exclusively as denunciation, to the detriment of other aspects of justice-seeking. Denunciations are spectacles that render a target's personal details visible in order to identify and vilify them. This comes at the expense of other necessary processes in justice-seeking, such as deliberation, judgement as well as assessment of proportionate punishment. With no due process and or presumption of innocence, the court of public opinion executes on sight. Even if one's good name is subsequently restored, damage to one's reputation may remain in the form of digital traces and collective memory linking the concerned target to the denunciation.

Individuals are the principal actors in scrutiny and denunciation, although governments and the media can enable or otherwise exert control over them. In contrast to most social movements and activism, they are also the principal targets of these interventions, as opposed to organisations, elective representatives or brands. We focus on both perpetrators and targets of mediated shaming, especially as people can easily experience both sides of online justice-seeking in the case of counter-denunciations. This book seeks to unpack scrutiny, denunciation and shaming as practices that are both historically and culturally situated, and augmented by digital media technologies, such that these practices intersect with domains like content creation and public relations. In doing so, it makes sense of contemporary visibility and what it means to be public-facing. In professional and personal life, people are compelled to be visible, transcending contexts that merge entertainment and commerce with discipline and justice. Most people lack adequate training or resources to cope with reputational fallout, especially as precarious workers and members of marginalised communities.

This book considers the tension between exceptional events like the response to the Charlottesville *Unite the Right* rally (Milbrandt, 2020), and mundane practices like shaming a neighbour for not disposing of their trash properly. Some incidents receive their own entries on sites like Wikipedia, Encyclopedia Dramatica and Know Your Meme, and shape discourse of acceptable practice. Others make up the daily landscape of disposable media consumption like rage scrolling. We address a dispersed collection of cultural phenomena on a global scale by examining cases occurring on digital platforms and legacy press, that in turn also reach audiences on digital platforms. Our analysis focuses primarily on events in Canada, China, the Netherlands, Russia, the UK and the US. These countries are culturally diverse, and some may seem to exhibit greater forms of authoritarianism. Yet we claim that the court of public opinion is a global phenomenon, with digitally mediated interventions found in and shaped by any given local context.

We provide an overview of mediated shaming related to #MeToo, anti-racist initiatives like Black Lives Matter (#BLM) and Stop Asian-American and Pacific Islander (AAPI) Hate, cancel culture and fan cultures, alongside the grievance media entrepreneurs who oversee a daily onslaught of denunciations. Some cases are situated in the context of the COVID-19 pandemic, which brought an expansion and amplification of weaponised data practices. Any one of these contexts warrants its own focus, which means we cannot provide a comprehensive account within these pages, nor can we sufficiently address every single concept that may be of relevance or of value to this topic. Instead, we draw attention to the exploitation of personal information in order to scrutinise, denounce and shame others, but also the processes by which these practices are made meaningful. The court of public opinion is composed of diverse actors. These include concerned individuals who can potentially reach a wide audience through viral content, professional content creators and influencers, digital platforms, legacy press and the state. Common to all these contexts and actors is the weaponised handling of the reputation of fellow civilians. We draw from an empirical base that includes both press and other media reports of online denunciation since 2006, as well as ninety-six interviews with participants and targets of online denunciation as well as those with a personal involvement or professional overview of these practices.

As many of these respondents either work in or are proximate to the media and tech sectors, they provide insights about the role and impact of digital media platforms in shaming practices. We are mindful of the ethical implications of public exposition of personal details, especially in instances where those people are involved in public shaming. As a result, we minimise the use of identifiable details in our writing.

New visibility as a longstanding condition

Public shaming practices are longstanding, with recent developments making them more visible and seemingly more persistent over time. There is diminishing reason to use the label 'new' when discussing new visibility, yet this term signals a continued acceleration and facilitation of accessing and processing personal information. New visibility refers to creating novel forms of interaction between social actors, including new kinds of utterances sent to public and private figures (Thompson, 2005, p. 32–33). These are broadly attributed to changes in technology, journalistic practice and political culture. Recent scholarship distinguishes between three modes of mediated visibility: broadcast, networked and algorithmic (Magalhães & Yu, 2022). While we focus primarily on networked forms of mediated visibility among audiences and social contacts, it remains that these three modes are entangled with each other in practice, and that "we have only begun to understand" this entanglement (ibid., p. 92).

In terms of venues, digital media platforms are "*more intensive*" due to greater content streams, "*more extensive*" due to increased recipients and "*less controllable*" due to a diminished "veil of secrecy" among politicians compared to prior forms of social scrutiny (Thompson, 2005, pp. 48–49; emphasis in original). Not only can we expect greater media engagement by unaffiliated people, but those who historically held greater control over their public image face new vulnerabilities. Consider the proliferation of websites that solicit and publish reviews of legal and dental professionals, among others.[9] Yet in practice these developments do not bring democratisation through surveillance: vulnerability through visibility is never equally applied (ibid., p. 42), especially as assessment of missteps is never impartially executed. Not only do denunciations reflect biases and vested interests, but those responding to accusations have unequal access to resources to protect their reputation. A privileged public figure like Donald Trump is routinely denounced, usually with credible evidence, and typically with little professional consequence. Meanwhile, a precarious worker may lose their job based on cynically or hastily interpreted content from their Twitter account. Popular claims of digital media visibility as transformative and empowering (Ariel et al., 2015; Rheingold, 2002) are contested when cultural, political and economic contexts shape post-revelatory conditions.

New forms of visibility can disrupt "normal appearances" due to revelations linked to domesticated media (Goldsmith 2010, p. 916). Civilians using smartphones to record police confrontations changed relations between police and the public. Maintaining a normal appearance that is free of scandal "is becoming more challenging for police and governments" (ibid., p. 917) as well as for civilians. In response, the target of denunciation (a police officer in this case) can invoke the broader context of their incident as a part of "repair work" (ibid., p. 926), such as offering the entire footage of a viral clip of police abuse, as a claim of an authoritative account. Yet these calls place demands on audiences in terms of bandwidth, mediation and attention that are seldom met. A 'broader context' that is incompatible with a fast-paced media environment can be cynically invoked to excuse police misconduct, even if a more detailed account would be even more damning to the officer. In polarised contexts, audiences may simply interpret the footage in a manner that reflects their worldview (Donovan et al., 2022).

There are instances when the court of public opinion is the only option for seeking justice amid dysfunctional or corrupt legal systems. Yet success stories tend to be outnumbered by cases of subsequent retaliation by authorities. A prime example is the Anti-Corruption Foundation in Russia (FBK) that actively exposes the Russian establishment and the wealth it amassed through corruption schemes. In these acts, FBK members relied on drone footage, open data sources and YouTube to gather their evidence and expose their targets, while also making themselves known to the public (Lokot, 2018). Yet the exposed politicians tend to enjoy a layer of immunity as they remain in power post-revelation, while many FBK members are either in prison or in exile.[10] Corruption-exposing activities may aid the political ambitions of activists, as was the case with FBK founder and, arguably, the most prominent opposition leader in post-Soviet Russia – Alexey Navalny. Navalny combined his political campaigning with the production of entertaining videos aimed at sparking populist fury among 'the people' who would protest after seeing how corrupt elites indulge in wealth. The plan did not work out for several reasons. First, most people in Russia either did not believe in the authenticity of such videos or did not have an issue with political leadership acquiring wealth.[11] Second, the state used politics of fear and its legislative capacities to deem such revelations extremist and erase them from public discourse. People were punished even retrospectively for their support of FBK in any form.[12] Third, the full-scale invasion of Ukraine redefined the playfield and unleashed the state's repressive machine. As such, Navalny was poisoned with a *Novichok* nerve agent in 2020, arrested in 2021, sentenced to nineteen years on charges of extremist activity in 2023 and eventually killed in the special regime colony in the Arctic Circle in 2024.

While many prominent cases of new visibility come from policing and politics, mediated scrutiny extends to interpersonal relations. Consider the perceived need to take action against crime and moral offences in cases lacking state support (Trottier, 2017). Taking justice into one's own hands is a crucial development, and it is paired with co-producing justice with an assemblage of (often imagined) others. This can be understood as a form of mediated vigilance (Trottier, 2020): the conditions in which audiences and digital media users are primed to watch over peers, perpetually reinforcing each other's behaviour. Audiences are a ubiquitous feature in digital media, and as part of this ubiquity they lack "reflexive visibility" (Girginova, 2016, p. 1) of their cultural and punitive impacts. Denunciation is thus normalised and made meaningful through deliberation about public figures like celebrities and influencers in popular discourse.

In looking at academic and popular accounts of mediated vigilance, we identify two forms of ambivalence. First, at a macro-level, denunciation and shaming can counter oppressive forms of gendered and racialised abuse, but can also be used to reproduce prevalent forms of discrimination. While 'cancel culture' is dismissed by critics as a left-wing practice, many of these critics employ the exact same tactic against progressive and marginalised targets. Second, at a micro-level, a denouncer may end up becoming the target of a separate denunciation based on their own misdeeds. In some cases, this may even be for the exact same type of misdeed.[13] This reflects a cultural expectation – or surveillant imaginary (Lyon, 2018; Kammerer, 2012) – that virtually everyone has misdeeds that can be discovered through an online search (cf. Trottier, 2018b).

Unpacking the court of public opinion

We use the term 'court of public opinion' not to fit all mediated social processes into a rigid legal framework, but to highlight how it operates parallel to conventional justice-seeking. We approach this term as a possible lens by considering elements that one may expect to find in the contexts-cum-jurisdictions that we cover in this book. Public opinion of individuals is shaped by how they are made visible through media. In framing user-centred deliberations as a kind of court of public opinion, it is helpful to briefly take stock of the contexts in which this term is invoked. Legal scholars use this term as a form of "legal spin control" (Moses, 1995, p. 1815), in which lawyers engage in mediated practices outside of court to shape the outcome of a court case. While typically working outside the public realm, here lawyers exert "increased advocacy" upon an engaged audience (ibid., 1813). Although this scholarship generally focuses on the judiciary (Stephenson, 2004), it is not just lawyers who manipulate public opinion, nor did they ever have a monopoly in the social contexts addressed below. We therefore focus on practices and outcomes occurring independently of legal practitioners. Even in court proceedings, vigilante media campaigns by non-judicial actors can influence sentencing.[14]

Public discourse surrounding the term 'court of public opinion' is no longer exclusive to courts of law. A recent editorial in *Medium* is entitled

"The court of public opinion is in session because the court of law sucks."[15] Such writing directs attention to the role of digital media users in denouncing others. Yet the current media landscape is also composed of established institutions that have historically shaped and asserted public opinion, including tabloids (Chadwick et al., 2018). Public opinion is constructed, not only by swaying or cultivating people's opinions through reporting, editorials and censorship, but also by populist political actors and other public figures asserting public opinion through highly visible broadcasts on behalf of 'the people' (Rooduijn, 2014). With the continued domestication of digital media, we see opinion-making as a strategy that is dispersed to diverse actors online.

Public opinion is (re)produced by (mis)informing people about other people's (mis)deeds. Yet it is also constructed through visibly and lastingly making the claim to the public, that the public has a firm opinion about them. In these cases, it is a matter of engaging media platforms to sway public opinion – and give the impression of a shifting public opinion – to win a court case or dispose of a political opponent. These are attempts to both engage with and shape a so-called public sphere, which has always been exclusionary of categories of individuals (Fraser, 1990), but also privately owned or influenced (Fuchs, 2014). Any democratising potential of a public sphere is compromised by built-in categorical discrimination that determines who is permitted to speak, how they may control their mediated visibility, as well as restrictions in terms of access and costs. In the context of digital media scrutiny, this includes mobilising diverse forms of capital within a social network (cf. Dupont, 2004).

This judicial imagery is fitting, as participants produce and circulate judgments against targets. Yet unlike actual courts, deliberations and (counter-) denunciations are increasingly visible and considered public in digital media practice. Cancellation has no contextual boundaries, but rather occurs in an approximation of the public sphere. It therefore comes as no surprise that these deliberations are typically housed on social media platforms that are privately owned approximations of a public sphere. This court also has no set roles, as seemingly anyone can attempt to serve as judge, jury, witness or lawyer. The notion of proportionality – the perceived fairness when measuring crime against punishment – is also called into question in these public trials. Applying the term 'court' to mediated scrutiny and denunciation underlines how justice-seeking coupled with entertainment adopts some judicial functions while eschewing others.

Denunciations clearly predate the internet. Yet the ways that they are mediated and understood suggest a decentralisation of calling people out that depends on digital platforms. Digital media users challenge a supposed monopolisation of sanction and violence by the state, but also the former exclusivity of the press for crime reporting and editorialising. These users may be independent of the police in principle, while fully dependent on digital platforms like Reddit and Facebook. Any sense of empowerment is inevitably shaped, mobilised and directed by platforms. This also underscores the tension between global and local: denunciations are an assertion of local grievances, values and expression. Yet they are filtered through and mediated by globally enforced "community standards" (Fiesler et al., 2018). Participants pick up on these standards, as well as appropriate signifiers, discourses and other communicative elements that transcend borders, in addition to media affordances (Treem & Leonardi, 2013) that enable a particular kind of information exchange that is also part of the learning curve. Denunciation, including cancellation, seems to be perpetually trialled (cf. Lehtonen, 2003) as acceptable social justice and entertainment media practices.

Judgment of others on digital platforms is often pre-emptive, as it is embedded in data gathering. Revelation of a misdeed seems to imply a verdict, unless someone contests the authenticity of content. In this context, the term 'receipt' refers to screenshots and other forms of incriminating content serving as authoritative digital artefacts. Receipts are legitimated across cultural contexts in terms of denunciation and justice-seeking. While it is reasonable to take seriously accusations accompanied by evidence, it also implies a migration of informal justice-seeking to a handful of digital platforms. Even embodied non-digital harms only become possible to denounce when there is a digital account. For example, consider the role of a blog post detailing sexual harassment that took place in a face-to-face setting.[16] Deliberation is largely pre-determined when invoking receipts. To question a denunciation by contemplating the broader context of an offence is itself often received by other media users as a defensive strategy, leading to further aggrievement. For this reason, we are not only interested in denunciation and verdicts, but also scrutiny and reputation management as ongoing pre-conditions on platform media. Routinised digital media data practices determine how individuals are seen by the world. Post-conditions matter as well, including imagined expectations of social life after being targeted and denounced. In cancel culture, digital media users explicitly state they want to ensure targets never work again in their current profession (Ng, 2022).

Revisiting status degradation ceremonies

Individuals being denounced serve as a source of moral indignation that bonds people together. At the same time, they are singled out and excluded, as "[f]or the collectivity shame is an individuator" (Garfinkel, 1956, p. 421). Mediated denunciations like being cancelled are attempts to lower the reputation of the target. They resemble what Garfinkel calls status degradation ceremonies. This refers to when one's social standing – how they are publicly known and the kind of social capital they can yield – is collectively reconfigured as much worse than previously imagined. In fact, given the lack of nuance in assessments of pedophiles, racists and even moderately asocial people, the target is often deemed to be abhorrent. Status degradation targets one's total identity (ibid., p. 420), imposing a motivational account of why the individual engages in misdeeds, rather than a specific account of how they behaved. Such attributions are thus difficult to verify or contest. In practice, people attribute contemptible traits to a target's inner core, even if there are more plausible explanations that do not circulate in a media frenzy, including the broader context, or simply the moments preceding the viral content. This speaks to the communicative power to influence audiences to accept these terms, or at least give the impression that a broader public has denounced the target.

Status degradation is also totalising in the sense that it transcends social context. Even if one acknowledges that the misdeed occurs in a specific set of circumstances, the way people talk about the target is not that they are a 'problematic entertainer' or an 'entertainer with problematic values' but rather the target is recognised as always having been problematic (ibid., pp. 421–422). There is the semblance of an uncovering: a revelation that gets at the true essence of the person (cf. Andrejevic, 2013), even in conceding that there is a context that is necessary to understand in order to make sense of the accused misdeed. For Garfinkel, the target of denunciation is often a public figure, for example when the political and economic elite in Chile are denounced via YouTube (Arancibia & Montecino, 2017). In addition, the denouncer must be recognised as a publicly known person (Garfinkel, 1956, p. 423). With #MeToo, anonymous accusations are often linked to and co-signed by a public media figure.[17] This is meant to ensure that the denouncer is not acting in private interest, but in their capacity as a public figure. On digital platforms, claims of instrumentalisation or 'making a career' of outrage is a frequent counterclaim against denunciations. A common tactic to dismiss sexual harassment and assault accusations in the Chinese #MeToo movement is to openly claim that the women involved are going public to garner fame (Ma, 2021). Yet it remains the case that both accusers and accused may gain prominence through online denunciation, whether as an unintended outcome or a deliberate attempt to launch a media career.

Historically the judicial system "and its officers have something like a fair monopoly over such ceremonies," to an extent that "they have become an occupational routine" (ibid., p. 424). While Garfinkel's focus was not on media, there are plenty of examples of personal reputations being downgraded through the press and television. The so-called 'perp walk' is a media ritual where the criminal justice system mobilises the press to make a suspect publicly visible, for example when taking them into a police station. The perp walk is a longstanding intersection of criminal justice and media spectacle (Bock, 2015). Yet these partnerships have also shifted from the public to the private sector with the advent of crime-fighting websites that label those with criminal records (Lageson & Maruna, 2018). Another global development is how these ceremonies are mainstreamed, privatised, seemingly handed over to digital media users. Status degradation spreads further to minor and decentralised media actors, who may be less inclined to uphold professional standards than the press or the police, yet are beholden to platform regulations. In terms of contemporary media power, individuals can denounce others, but depend on a range of other actors for such accusations to hold, including journalists, platform operators and public relations professionals. At the same time what we witness on Reddit and elsewhere are not orthodox degradation ceremonies, but more routinised and pervasive media rituals designed to engage audiences.

On reputation as depletable

Reputation as a concept is dispersed and intangible, especially as it is shaped by external perception (Solove, 2007). This intangibility is not meant to diminish its social relevance. Rather, it means that perception can extend from vague and unconfirmed rumours to "social death" confirmed by an assemblage of individuals, media platforms and states (Huang, 2022, p. 16). Like a lot of concepts in this book, reputation is especially palpable when it is compromised. In fact, stories of privacy violations often include damaged reputations, as when sensitive content from private conversations is made public.[18]

In working with a flexible definition of reputation, we can first distinguish between the reputation of an individual, and the reputation of a media platform, employer or brand. While this book concerns individual reputation, the relationship between corporate reputation and the reputation of current, former and future employees is a growing concern. We can also distinguish between a descriptive approach to reputation (*What are you known for?*) and a normative approach (*Are you tainted as a public figure? Do you have skeletons in your closet?*). These are two prevailing and seemingly compatible understandings of reputation. The first is reputation as a project of connection and prominence that is largely synonymous with cultivating a rich and high-performing social network. This is measured not only in terms of high ratings, but high engagement metrics more generally, particularly in creative and media industries (Hearn, 2010). This is reputation understood as a brand (Gandini & Pais, 2020) or score (Citron & Pasquale, 2014), although the evaluative dimension of a score slips towards a second and more normative understanding of reputation. Reputation is a matter of being known to the public, and known to make an impact, especially in the context of a short-term news cycle that can in turn be exploited for further derivative content and engagements. Yet from status degradation ceremonies we can also understand reputation in a negative sense as the absence of stigma (Goffman, 1968). Here reputation is practically a vacuum waiting to be occupied, or a blank slate that serves as a precursor to imminent scandal, stigma and shame. Positive or even neutral reputation appears to be fleeting, especially in contemporary media environments. This understanding is resonant with – but not exclusive to – honour cultures (Pearce & Vitak, 2016): one's reputation and the reputations of those close to them are vulnerable, and having them compromised brings lasting and totalising consequences. Such an understanding of reputation is measured tangibly by a search engine query that does not yield any scandalous results, even if the term 'allegations' is added to the query.

Reputation as both a project and a vulnerability seems fitting when talking about former reality television participants who are compromised on camera, and then continue to seek media work by circulating through less prestigious appearances at nightclubs.[19] These figures pass through a programme where they are set up to have a tarnished reputation (Palmer, 2006), and are then left to earn a living by working with that tarnished reputation. They have crossed a threshold of being stigmatised and discredited, yet their reputation is still a driving force for media work. We can seemingly tell a similar story about vloggers, influencers, SoundCloud musicians, young adult authors, podcasters, comedians, cultural critics and other forms of work that involve being visible through one or multiple platforms. In broader job settings, temporary contracts mean that mobilising one's social network is vital for future viability. This speaks to an existential condition for public-facing individuals in which they may feel a need to stand out for their next paycheque. In turn, this leads to prescriptions about professional networks as ever-expanding through weak ties, which in turn facilitate leaks and other kinds of diffusion.

This kind of measurable reputation can apply to individuals as entrepreneurial selves, but also to platforms or brands. People measure prominent figures' performance in terms of key metrics. They invoke similar metrics when arguing about the importance of TikTok or Nike in their respective sectors. As we will see in Chapter 4, reputation is especially understood as depletable when exploited in engagement economies of digital media platforms. Reputation is partly imagined in terms of connection and engagement. Yet engagement is often controversial, such that mobilising as a prominent figure on a digital platform is risky, whether as leisure or labour. There seems to be an implicit assumption in media practice that audiences wish to consume the misdeeds and thus the reputation of others.

Shaming and contemporary media cultures

Contemporary media practices treat reputations as a raw material to exploit – be it for the purpose of justice-seeking or sheer entertainment. Scholars like Solove reflect on how personal reputations have been processed at the turn of the 21st century, through a broader population adopting the internet in daily life. The early 2000s saw an expansion of websites such as those creating "blacklists of individuals who file medical malpractice claims" (Solove, 2007, p. 98). In this case, legal mechanisms against malpractice are compromised through an informal counter-denunciation website. Just as overt surveillance has a chilling effect on public expression, such websites inhibit claimants from seeking formal redress.

Being public-facing now refers to any job in a public or service sector, including interacting with the public at a cash register. Yet it increasingly also applies to any sort of mediated reachability, searchability and accountability that extends beyond the hours and spaces in which someone is working. People get in trouble for not knowing the often-unspoken rules in social settings, leading to exposure and denunciation (ibid., p. 39). These rules are prescriptions about proper conduct, but more directly rules about proper data handling. These are acknowledged more explicitly in certain media professions, including knowing what a 'hot mic' is, what counts as 'on the record,' what is a reasonable expectation of privacy. Much like today, the early 2000s can be framed as a period of reputation-management catching up with technological realities. A media-savvy person may have the awareness to mind what they write in an email but neglect to appreciate how the location data their mobile device gives off may also be used against them in a public denunciation. The public may still blame these people for not knowing better, and their stories may become embedded in surveillant imaginaries that make sense of these rules.[20] It is also worth underlining how people suffer damaged reputations because of voluntary media practices like blogging, webcamming and participation in reality television. Cultures of confession (Aslama & Pantti, 2006) often serve as a necessary counterpart to voyeuristic audiences.

Earlier writing on status degradation and online reputation suggests a need to focus more on the actors involved and the disparities they face in terms of capital and social privilege. The discourse of free data and empowerment in Solove's work appears to downplay this inequality. Scrutiny and denunciation build on a range of conditions of having information accessible to and on anyone in the public domain, but also from semi-public and even private spaces. Framing information as free (Solove, 2007, pp. 3–4) overlooks material costs and unequal access to diverse forms of capital. Google is more affordable than hiring a private investigator, but the person who can afford the latter has both the private investigator and search engine (cf. ibid., p. 9). And reputation continues to be a volatile concept in practice because of new conditions of being public-facing as a necessity, as when a worker regularly posts personal content to their own YouTube account out of professional obligation. They may accumulate followers in the process. At what point (e.g. garnering over a hundred 'likes' per post) do people start to think of themselves as public-facing, having significant social 'clout' and being an 'influencer'?

We need to consider information management processes that are now mainstreamed. Similar media practices, attitudes and rhetorics are manifest in different contexts across a broader media landscape. Studying the court of public opinion is important due to the persistent solicitation of feedback across institutional settings, an ever-expanding quantification of online interactions (e.g. getting 'ratioed'[21]) and the manner in which these data practices reinforce existing injustices such as discrimination. These are not always the driving forces that compel people to watch and be watched by their peers, but they add to the social significance and impact of these practices. Anybody not independently wealthy is likely concerned with their place in the labour market, such that this may be compromised if they are a target of mediated denunciation.

Prominence in digital media is only the most recent iteration of public self-management. These practices become explicit and necessary strategies, and the idea of the self is further managed as a commodity. This manifests as promotionalism (Wernick, 1991) and enterprise culture (du Gay & Salaman, 1992) that compel individuals to maintain a strategic distrust in language and engage in self-promotion that emphasises actions, both one's own good deeds, but also the misdeeds of others. In digital media cultures, it becomes even easier for others to contest and intervene against one's self-promotion. Market pressures compel a perpetual "personal visibility campaign" (Hearn, 2008, p. 205), where being public-facing is a strategy, accompanied by an inherent risk of harmful exposure in many job sectors. Care for one's own public personal standing leads to a context where people process the risks they (and others) face and can put these to use in cases where they intervene in the lives of others for purposes of justice, entertainment or harm.

Chapter overview

The next four chapters each address a particular set of actors that participate in the court of public opinion. While we describe mediated denunciation and shaming as user-led, media platforms and states are often key beneficiaries of these practices.

Chapter 2 focuses on seemingly ordinary people who denounce and are denounced by others. While high-profile individuals are often involved in such cases, we start by focusing on these less prominent media users. These concerned individuals report on a wide range of minor offences, including dog feces in public spaces and plagiarism among content creators. These relations bring a duality of mediated visibility, as anybody can watch over others while also beholden to their gaze. After a brief exploration of historical contexts, we offer an empirical account of mediated shaming through interviews with those engaged in these practices, including journalists, data scientists, academics and knowledge workers. Drawing on their first-hand experiences denouncing and being denounced, we address how individuals cope with mediated shaming in their professional as well as personal lives. While these incidents occur in localised contexts, a common finding across countries is how cultural polarisation amplifies online strife. These experiences inform how participants make sense of watching and being watched by others, as well as personal consequences of exposure and denunciation.

Chapter 3 spotlights how prominent users become entangled in online scrutiny and shaming. This includes influencers and content creators who establish followings in the millions, but also those who labour in the hundreds or thousands. Theirs is a visibility in which reputation and legitimacy are continuously built up and contested. High follower counts are a pathway to capital, power and privilege. Yet they may remain vulnerable to attacks on their reputation precisely because of this prominence. We offer a close reading of cancel culture discourse as polarising and contested. In practice, it typically amounts to an ideological curation of grievances. We introduce the notion of prominence as an attribute that helps make sense of contemporary regimes of visibility in media and entertainment. This informs a broader discussion of cancel culture as both a tangible media practice and a selective framing of incidents. We contend that public discourse about cancel culture effectively becomes a "moral panic about moral panics" (Cree et al., 2016, p. 355; Cohen, 2011). This framing enables us to consider routinised denunciation as both productive for media engagement and damaging to the reputations of those attaining prominence.

Chapter 4 focuses on platforms where digital shaming occurs. Digital media are easily taken for granted due to their ubiquity in personal and professional lives, yet they serve as ideologically-tinted windows to the world for many people. This reliance is especially acute in cases of social isolation, whether due to public health emergencies or cultural polarisation. With a co-constructivist approach to media technologies, we understand platforms as both instrumentalised by their user base and operating in the service of owners for financial gain and cultural influence. We therefore approach the court of public opinion as a synthesis of engagement and reputation economies. Platforms operate as spaces that cultivate and contain reputational practices. This now includes repurposing platforms like Yelp and TripAdvisor to 'review bomb' targets with fraudulent one-star reviews.[22] Our respondents describe a troubling dependence on platforms that also leads to volatility in terms of visibility and reputational harm. These struggles shape users' sense of belonging to – and exclusion from – social platforms. Reflecting on user experiences with these platforms leads to a practical reconsideration of notions of consent to exposure. These practical reflections in turn shape more fundamental understandings of ethics and harm through digital platforms.

In Chapter 5 we shift our focus to states, including politicians, police and public servants. State scrutiny and control over populations are both challenged and enhanced by digitisation. Here our analysis troubles assumptions that user-led practices and states' use of media are mutually exclusive. As a point of departure, we consider cases where politicians make appeals to audiences to watch over and report antisocial behaviour among civilians, including in public health contexts, political polarisation (e.g. so-called 'leftist indoctrination'), but also in more mundane and routine incidents. We assert that shame-based assemblages can serve state agendas, with unanticipated outcomes and offshoots. Yet states can openly distance themselves from initiatives they implicitly support and from which they may benefit. Civilians are at the same time an extension of and a liability for the state. The 'court of public opinion' invoked by civilians through platforms is both a tool for the state and at times beyond state control. We spotlight China and Russia as models of state involvement in and influence over civilian practices. This provides insights towards how to globally frame and analyse state policies towards online shitstorms in the coming years.

The last chapter advances an interdisciplinary and cross-sector focus to understand the digitally mediated mobilisation of status degradation. We provide a summative account of the empirical and conceptual contributions from the first five chapters. This allows us to consider the interlinked dependencies between various actors involved in so-called online shitstorms. While it is tempting to reduce these instances to a single type of media user (like online mobs) or a single political context (like social justice warriors), the entanglements we see between various types of media users, platforms and states suggest a global tendency to disrupt social sanction. The court of public opinion offers a conceptual framework to address how diverse contexts make use of converging media. We conclude with key tensions and directions for subsequent research, noting how mediated shaming processes are either absorbed by prominent polarising trends or rendered invisible as implicit and unspoken forms of social control. We also identify empirical areas of study that signal emerging types of accounts, platforms and practices.

Notes

1. To a lesser extent, 'covidiot' is also used to describe people who follow public health protocols. This divergence is seen among the hundreds of user-generated definitions for covidiot on UrbanDictionary, and this speaks to how new denunciatory terms will be used in a deeply polarised manner: https://www.urbandictionary.com/define.php?term=Covidiot
2. https://nypost.com/2020/04/02/covidiot-blogger-arielle-charnas-may-have-ruined-her-brand/
3. https://twitter.com/karaswisher/status/1247016530799472643
4. While writing this book, Twitter was acquired by Elon Musk and rebranded as X. Nevertheless, we use the term Twitter to maintain consistency with our interview respondents, who refer to the platform by its original name.
5. https://twitter.com/charliekirk11/status/1241820673007161345
6. https://foreignpolicy.com/2009/05/19/the-brave-new-world-of-slacktivism/
7. Doxing refers to a digital media practice where malicious actors publish personal and sensitive information about a target, see Douglas (2016).
8. https://sandyandnora.com/episode-8-from-me-too-us-the-limits-of-the-me-too-movement/ (19:50–21:15)
9. See blog posts that direct attention to a wide range of such review platforms, such as https://www.repugen.com/blog/dentist-review-sites and https://www.nivancontent.com/lawyer-review-sites/
10. https://www.opendemocracy.net/en/odr/alexey-navalny-russia-opposition-leader-new-trial-prison-putin/
11. https://www.themoscowtimes.com/2021/02/08/1-in-4-russians-watched-navalnys-putin-palace-investigation-poll-a72861
12. https://www.rferl.org/a/russia-navalny-leaked-data/31416321.html

13 See for example a set of American politicians denounced for antisemitism after denouncing the antisemitism of their rivals: https://twitter.com/JewishWorker/status/1095065455641980932
14 https://socialmediadna.nl/kopschoppers/
15 https://medium.com/@benmcc.writing/the-court-of-public-opinion-is-in-session-because-the-court-of-law-sucks-2f385cbf8be3
16 https://babe.net/2018/01/13/aziz-ansari-28355
17 See example from previous footnote: https://babe.net/2018/01/13/aziz-ansari-28355
18 In the case of past problematic tweets, the notion of a privacy violation is complicated. It may be the case that the tweets in question were already accessible, such that they are somewhat amplified in the revelation. It may also be the case that they were deleted, in which case their resurfacing would likely be experienced as further troubling.
19 https://www.gawker.com/5516209/the-bizarre-world-of-reality-tv-nightclub-appearances: "We don't have any special talents other than selling ourselves."
20 See for instance prominent examples like Dooced, #HasJustineLandedYet and Milkshake Duck.
21 When a reply to a post gets more positive feedback such as 'likes' and 'upvotes' than the post itself, a digital media user may attempt to 'ratio' the author of the post to demonstrate that public sentiment does not favour the poster and their viewpoints.
22 For example, Yelp users submitted one-star reviews on the practice of a dentist who hunted and killed a lion in Zimbabwe: https://www.wired.com/2015/07/yelp-poacher/

References

Andrejevic, M. (2007).*iSpy: Surveillance and power in the interactive era*. University Press of Kansas. https://doi.org/10.2307/jj.11634956

Andrejevic, M. (2013). *Infoglut: How too much information is changing the way we think and know*. Routledge. https://doi.org/10.4324/9780203075319

Arancibia, M. C., & Montecino, L. (2017). The construction of anger in comments on the public behavior of members of the social elite in Chile. *Discourse & Society*, *28*(6), 595–613. https://doi.org/10.1177/0957926517721084

Ariel, B., Farrar, W. A., & Sutherland, A. (2015). The effect of police body-worn cameras on use of force and citizens' complaints against the police: A randomized controlled trial. *Journal of Quantitative Criminology*, *31*, 509–535. https://doi.org/10.1007/s10940-014-9236-3

Aslama, M., & Pantti, M. (2006). Talking alone: Reality TV, emotions and authenticity. *European Journal of Cultural Studies*, *9*(2), 167–184. https://doi.org/10.1177/1367549406063162

Bergemann, P. (2017). Denunciation and social control. *American Sociological Review*, *82*(2), 384–406. https://doi.org/10.1177/0003122417694456

Bock, M. A. (2015). Framing the accused: The perp walk as media ritual. *Visual Communication Quarterly*, *22*(4), 206–220. https://doi.org/10.1080/15551393.2015.1105104

Cai, D. A., & Tolan, C. (2020). Public shaming and attacks on social media: The case of White evangelical Christians. *Negotiation and Conflict Management Research*, *13*(3), 231–243. https://doi.org/10.1111/ncmr.12188

Chadwick, A., Vaccari, C., & O'Loughlin, B. (2018). Do tabloids poison the well of social media? Explaining democratically dysfunctional news sharing. *New Media & Society*, *20*(11), 4255–4274. https://doi.org/10.1177/1461444818769689

Citron, D. K., & Pasquale, F. (2014). The scored society: Due process for automated predictions. *Washington Law Review*, *89*(1), 1–34.

Cohen, S. (2011). Whose side were we on? The undeclared politics of moral panic theory. *Crime, Media, Culture*, *7*(3), 237–243. https://doi.org/10.1177/1741659011417603

Clark, M. D. (2020). DRAG THEM: A brief etymology of so-called "cancel culture". *Communication and the Public*, *5*(3–4), 88–92. https://doi.org/10.1177/2057047320961562

Cree, V. E., Clapton, G., & Smith, M. (2016). Standing up to complexity: Researching moral panics in social work.*European Journal of Social Work*, *19*(3–4), 354–367. https://doi.org/10.4324/9781315206929-5

Donovan, J., Dreyfuss, E., & Friedberg, B. (2022). *Meme wars: The untold story of the online battles upending democracy in America*. Bloomsbury Publishing.

Douglas, D. M. (2016). Doxing: A conceptual analysis. *Ethics and Information Technology*, *18*(3), 199–210. https://doi.org/10.1007/s10676-016-9406-0

Du Gay, P., & Salaman, G. (1992). The cult[ure] of the customer. *Journal of Management Studies*, *29*(5), 615–633. https://doi.org/10.1111/j.1467-6486.1992.tb00681.x

Dupont, B. (2004). Security in the age of networks. *Policing and Society*, *14*(1), 76–91. https://doi.org/10.1080/1043946042000181575

Enzweiler, M. J. (2014). Swatting political discourse: A domestic terrorism threat. *Notre Dame Legal Review*, *90*(5), 2001–2038. https://scholarship.law.nd.edu/ndlr/vol90/iss5/9

Fiesler, C., Jiang, J., McCann, J., Frye, K., & Brubaker, J. (2018). Reddit rules! characterizing an ecosystem of governance. In *Proceedings of the International AAAI Conference on Web and Social Media, 12*(1), 72–81. https://doi.org/10.1609/icwsm.v12i1.15033

Fraser, N. (1990). Rethinking the public sphere: A contribution to the critique of actually existing democracy. *Social Text*, (25/26), 56–80. https://doi.org/10.2307/466240

Fuchs, C. (2014). Social media and the public sphere. *TripleC: Communication, Capitalism & Critique. Open Access Journal for a Global Sustainable Information Society*, *12*(1), 57–101. https://doi.org/10.31269/triplec.v12i1.552

Gandini, A., & Pais, I. (2020). Reputation and personal branding in the platform economy. In S. Taylor & S. Luckman (Eds.), *Pathways into creative working lives*(pp. 231–248). Palgrave Macmillan. https://doi.org/10.1007/978-3-030-38246-9_13

Garfinkel, H. (1956). Conditions of successful degradation ceremonies. *American Journal of Sociology*, *61*(5), 420–424. https://doi.org/10.1086/221800

Girginova, K. (2016). The disappearing audience and reflexive visibility. *Social Media + Society*, *2*(3), 1–3. https://doi.org/10.1177/2056305116662172

Goffman, E. (1968). *Stigma: Notes on the management of spoiled identity*. Simon and Schuster.

Goldsmith, A. J. (2010). Policing's new visibility. *The British Journal of Criminology*, *50*(5), 914–934. https://doi.org/10.1093/bjc/azq033.

Hearn, A. (2008). 'Meat, mask, burden': Probing the contours of the branded 'self'. *Journal of Consumer Culture*, *8*(2), 197–217. https://doi.org/10.1177/1469540508090086

Hearn, A. (2010). Structuring feeling: Web 2.0, online ranking and rating, and the digital 'reputation' economy. *Ephemera: Theory & Politics in Organization*, *10*(3/4), 421–438.

Huang, Q. (2022). *The assemblage of social death: Mapping vigilantism in China. PhD Dissertation*. Erasmus University Rotterdam.

Kammerer, D. (2012). Surveillance in literature, film and television. In K. Ball, K. Haggerty, & D. Lyon (Eds.), *Routledge handbook of surveillance studies* (pp. 99–106). Routledge. https://doi.org/10.4324/9780203814949.ch1_3_c

Lageson, S. E., & Maruna, S. (2018). Digital degradation: Stigma management in the internet age.*Punishment & Society*, *20*(1), 113–133. https://doi.org/10.1177/1462474517737050

Lehtonen, T. K. (2003). The domestication of new technologies as a set of trials. *Journal of Consumer Culture*, *3*(3), 363–385. https://doi.org/10.1177/14695405030033014

Lokot, T. (2018). Be safe or be seen? How Russian activists negotiate visibility and security in online resistance practices. *Surveillance and Society*, *16*(3), 332–346. https://doi.org/10.24908/ss.v16i3.6967

Lyon, D. (2018). *The culture of surveillance: Watching as a way of life*. Wiley & Sons.

Ma, L. (2021). *#MeToo and cyber activism in China: Gendered violence and scripts of power*. Routledge. https://doi.org/10.4324/9781003197782

Magalhães, J. V., & Yu, J. (2022). Mediated visibility and recognition: A taxonomy. In A. Brighenti (Ed.), *The new politics of visibility spaces: Actors, practices and technologies in the visible* (pp. 72–99). Intellect. https://doi.org/10.1386/9781789385748

Marwick, A. E. (2021). Morally motivated networked harassment as normative reinforcement. *Social Media + Society*, *7*(2). https://doi.org/10.1177/20563051211021378

Milbrandt, T. (2020). 'Make them famous': Digital vigilantism and virtuous denunciation after Charlottesville. In D. Trottier, R. Gabdulhakov, & Q. Huang (Eds.), *Introducing vigilant audiences* (pp. 215–258). Open Book Publishers. https://doi.org/10.11647/obp.0200.09

Moses, J. M. (1995). Legal spin control: Ethics and advocacy in the court of public opinion. *Columbia Law Review*, *95*(7), 1811–1856. https://doi.org/10.2307/1123196

Ng, E. (2022). *Cancel culture: A critical analysis*. Palgrave Macmillan. https://doi.org/10.1007/978-3-030-97374-2

Palmer, G. (2006). Video vigilantes and the work of shame. *Jump Cut: A Review of Contemporary Media*, *48*(1). https://www.ejumpcut.org/archive/jc48.2006/shameTV/text.html

Pearce, K. E., & Vitak, J. (2016). Performing honor online: The affordances of social media for surveillance and impression management in an honor culture.*New Media & Society*, 18(11), 2595–2512. https://doi.org/10.1177/1461444815600279

Rheingold, H. (2002). *Smart mobs: The next social revolution*. Basic Books.

Rooduijn, M. (2014). The nucleus of populism: In search of the lowest common denominator. *Government and Opposition*, *49*(4), 573–599. https://doi.org/10.1017/gov.2013.30

Solove, D. J. (2007).*The future of reputation: Gossip, rumor, and privacy on the internet*. Yale University Press. https://doi.org/10.12987/9780300138191

Stephenson, M. C. (2004). Court of public opinion: Government accountability and judicial independence. *Journal of Law, Economics, and Organization*, *20*(2), 379–399. https://doi.org/10.1093/jleo/ewh038

Thompson, J. B. (2005). The new visibility. *Theory, Culture & Society*, *22*(6), 31–51. https://doi.org/10.1177/0263276405059413

Treem, J. W., & Leonardi, P. M. (2013). Social media use in organizations: Exploring the affordances of visibility, editability, persistence, and association. *Annals of the International Communication Association*, *36*(1), 143–189. https://doi.org/10.1080/23808985.2013.11679130

Trottier, D. (2017). Digital vigilantism as weaponisation of visibility. *Philosophy & Technology*, *30*, 55–72. https://doi.org/10.1007/s13347-016-0216-4

Trottier, D. (2018a). Coming to terms with shame: Exploring mediated visibility against transgressions. *Surveillance and Society*, *16*(2), 170-182. https://doi.org/10.24908/ss.v16i2.6811

Trottier, D. (2018b). Scandal mining: Political nobodies and remediated visibility. *Media, Culture & Society*, *40*(6), 893–908. https://doi.org/10.1177/0163443717734408

Trottier, D. (2020). Denunciation and doxing: Towards a conceptual model of digital vigilantism. *Global Crime*, *21*(3–4), 196–212. https://doi.org/10.1080/17440572.2019.1591952

Tuerkheimer, D. (2019). Beyond #MeToo. *NYU Law Review*, *94*, 1146–1208.

Wernick, A. (1991). Promotional culture. *CTheory*, *15*(1–3), 260–281. https://journals.uvic.ca/index.php/ctheory/article/view/14281

Yin, S., & Sun, Y. (2021). Intersectional digital feminism: assessing the participation politics and impact of the MeToo movement in China. *Feminist Media Studies*, *21*(7), 1176–1192. http://doi.org/10.1080/14680777.2020.1837908

2 Concerned individuals as participants and targets of shaming

Local, proximate and meaningful denunciation

Media shaming is often centred on prominent incidents that generate engagement, such as high-profile crimes, racist violence or child sexual exploitation. Many cases involve celebrities, public figures or otherwise highly recognisable individuals. Yet mediated scrutiny and denunciation are also tools used by – and against – unaffiliated and otherwise low-profile individuals. These practices are routinised as seemingly unremarkable processes in which people watch over and denounce their peers. Consider one of our interviewees combating the problem of dog feces in parks and on sidewalks. As a concerned individual in the UK, she developed an app for residents to publish reports of animal waste in public spaces. She was motivated by frustrations that people in her neighbourhood regularly face, including young children stepping in filth. Not only does this initiative serve the local public, the person responsible also made these resources available to other communities with instructions on how to export the service.

In another case, a US-based freelance writer denounced a plagiarist in his community, and reflected on this offence and denunciation in a published article. Instead of concerning a local neighbourhood, 'local interests' can be understood as linked to a professional network. Denunciation here is in service of a community of writers, given their precarious working conditions and risk of being plagiarised. While this scrutiny and denunciation take place online, they are no less crucial to their material existence. Subculture communities account for another type of 'local' and platforms can also make them visible outside of their circles, which can lead to offence-taking and denunciation. In China, a collective of content creators and other netizens named *The 227 United* publicly denounced an actor's fans for endangering freedom of expression (Huang et al., 2023). This incident was triggered by the shutdown of the fanfiction platform *Archive of Our Own* (AO3) in China because of a report to government authorities made by Xiao Zhan's fans. This report takes issue with a fan fiction featuring Xiao Zhan as a prostitute with dysphoria. *The 227 United* regarded the shutdown of AO3 as the loss of a haven for creative works. In addition to targeting his fans, they cancelled Xiao by giving low reviews to Xiao-related products.[1]

DOI: 10.4324/9781003453017-2

These cases concern the mobilisation of local publics, understood as communities sharing a geographic space or cultural interests (cf. Kudaibergenova, 2020). While the UK-based app developer wanted to preserve clean streets and other public spaces, the US-based freelance writer sought to preserve the economic viability and recognition of his labour. In the Chinese example, vigilant fan communities wanted to preserve their cultural practice amid a hostile media landscape. Local public communities matter because of their proximity, common interests and shared vulnerabilities. This chapter addresses how unaffiliated individuals scrutinise and denounce other people, focusing on their motivations, perceptions, regrets and recommendations. We seek to make sense of the overlap between terms like user and citizen, as well as those excluded from these labels. Increasingly, citizenship is performed through the use of media platforms and devices (Hintz et al., 2017). It is thus configured by platform logics (Andersson Schwarz, 2017) that shape user practice. This chapter also contributes to unpacking the notion of justice-seeking: how concerned individuals see themselves in the context of mediated practices and justify their behaviour. We focus on cases where individuals seek to address and remedy illegal and immoral activity in their immediate vicinity, through digitally mediated denunciation. They are typically motivated by a mix of principles like social justice and tangible threats to their livelihood or well-being.

When calling these people unaffiliated, we mean that they may belong to professional networks, but are not acting on behalf of formal organisations like the press, government or private companies. At most, we may see a loose clustering of people united by a cause. Thus, these events appear to be more predominantly shaped by peer-to-peer relations. These individuals routinely cope with watching over others, and being watched over by others (cf. Trottier, 2012). This chapter thus concerns people both denouncing and being denounced. Our interviews reveal that any single individual is often struggling with both, especially as expressing grievances can bring public backlash. Becoming publicly facing to denounce someone may lead to counter-denunciation. This chapter extends from the literature on peer surveillance that responds to a potential flattening of the field of social visibility. Under these conditions not only can anyone watch over peers and strangers, they also run the risk of becoming a target of someone else's scrutiny. These developments extend from what Haggerty and Ericson (2000, p. 606) call a "leveling of the hierarchy of surveillance": due to several socio-cultural and technological factors, we are witnessing a scaling up of peer scrutiny and denunciation. Yet shaming processes and outcomes continue to reflect social inequality and injustices. Those who wield privilege and capital can endure mediated shaming better than those at the margins.

Since the early days of social media, lateral surveillance extends from close friendships and romances, to persons of interest like potential roommates, to strangers encountered online (Marwick, 2012). This expansion of targets of mediated scrutiny informs a broader sensemaking process (cf. Louis, 1980) in which digital media users discover the opportunities and risks for watching and being watched made possible by social media and mobile device ubiquity, along with the implementation of other domestic surveillance infrastructures like dashcams and smart doorbells. This sensemaking is in turn linked to other relations of visibility, denunciation and reputational harm described in later chapters. These practices are anchored in – and made meaningful by – technical features, but also by local contexts. Local conditions shape how denunciation unfolds, be they regional or those of a particular community or subculture. This is accomplished by linking the personal data and reputation of targeted people to a given territory. Amsterdam's inner city is made knowable through photos and other content about tourists, landlords and other 'antisocial' threats.[2] Portland, Oregon is made knowable through user-shared footage of carjackers and drug users.[3] A small residential community in Shanghai is made knowable through the shared security footage of a man abusing cats.[4] Because local offline spaces are made visible through online global platforms, we recognise that these two binaries are coupled in practice. Beyond geographic proximity, a freelance writing community may be understood – internally and by outsiders – through prominent internet shaming shitstorms featuring members of their community. Targeting, denunciation and shaming are also transboundary activities, often informed by prejudice and bias. The consequent shaming may extend to other contexts in which the target is based, for example when grievances within the young adult fiction community are mainstreamed to a wider audience.[5] A more vivid example of transboundary harm is the exposure and retaliation against exposure of Kyrgyz women working in Russia by fellow male compatriots. Male migrants take offence when they see Kyrgyz women in public with men of other ethnic groups. Feeling that the women betray their motherland through such activities, male migrants assault them physically and in a sexualised manner while filming the process. By sharing the footage online, concerned individuals ensure that their community back home participates in the shaming process. As a result of such transnational retaliation, targeted women find it nearly impossible to return home while seeking legal justice in Russia is a hopeless and potentially dangerous endeavour (Gabdulhakov, 2019).

Accounting for active citizens and civilians

We briefly consider some localised contexts in which people watch other individuals in a sustained and organised manner. Even in a restricted overview we recognise distinctions between socially progressive and regressive cases, while also noting the gradual inclusion of digital tools to supplement these practices. In Western digitally mediated contexts, the so-called 'norm police' play an important role in reproducing and enforcing local morality. Solove (2007, p. 6) refers to the norm police as the "few folks" who are essential to upholding common values. As an example of emerging social ills that require policing, Solove cites being loud on mobile phones in public (ibid., p. 86). More recent social ills include hate speech on Twitter aimed at public figures and private individuals (Douglas, 2020). Digital media are not just new means to denounce offences, but also the venues where these offences take place. The norm police are specific people who are coupled with a broader audience they mobilise, making their denunciation socially impactful. This suggests a pattern of a few people who may take the initiative, who in practice are inextricable from a larger audience or following who witness these steps. We may consider what the rest of the population is doing if only 'few folks' are policing norms. This broader audience contributes to mediated shaming by bearing witness to events, generating viewer metrics in the process. In addition to being compelled to play a minor role in generating content through (re)posting and commenting, by adding to digital media view and subscriber counts, they also reinforce the presence of an imagined audience.

In addition to historical accounts of informal justice-seeking within communities (Dobash & Dobash, 1981) we can consider more recent global iterations from the twentieth century. Neighbourhood watch schemes in countries like the US and UK exemplify pre-internet precedents of citizen crime fighting and norm policing. These emerged to some degree due to top-down appeals from political figures like Margaret Thatcher (Moores, 2017), a point we explore further in Chapter 5. Here, citizens are expected to watch over local spaces and notify authorities as well as each other in case of suspicious activity. These initiatives are criticised based on individual and administrative approach to public security, thus excluding those who do not own property (ibid.). In recent years, these initiatives have extended to digital platforms with the predominance of over ten thousand WhatsApp *Buurtpreventie* [neighbourhood watch] groups in the Netherlands, who police security threats as well as minor irritants. Here we witness a slipping into norm policing that is facilitated by top-down initiatives at a national level,[6] including guidelines for police involvement.[7] Yet these groups also emerge organically when civilians decide to launch a local branch.

In Russia, civilian-led scrutiny against neighbours resembles the Soviet-era practices of communal policing (Gabdulhakov, 2018). The founder of the Soviet state, Vladimir Lenin, even envisioned a society where the police would wither away as citizens driven by communist morality would police each other (Kucherov, 1970). This vision incarnated in the form of so-called 'comrade courts' where Soviet citizens would publicly shame each other over minor grievances. A ubiquitous snitching culture allowed people to report each other to police and secret service for acting in a non-communist manner by, for instance, listening to Western music, wearing jeans or chewing gum. Given this history in Russia, the idea that citizens must be concerned and actively manage each other was not alien when it reincarnated once again in the form of digital vigilantism in the mid-2000s. As we see below, this arguably began with a neo-Nazi movement using digital media to spread its ideology while attracting vast audiences to the 'spectacle of punishment' of digitally mediated public humiliation.

The legacy of community management in China is also carried to the digital era. During the cultural revolution, Chinese citizens were encouraged by the party-state to monitor each other's daily activities and expose their wrongdoings in *pidoudahui* [批斗大会, struggle sessions] or directly to the party committee. The triggers of these reports and struggle sessions varied from political stances to romantic relationships, which were less of a reflection of authentic public opinion but more directed by the party-state ideology. However, monitoring fellow citizens, reporting their wrongdoings and publicly shaming the perceived perpetrators became key practices for Chinese citizens (Gorman, 2017).

When it comes to watching over local terrains, we observe global trends where civilians engage in vigilance in public transportation (Trottier et al., 2020) as well as monitoring misconduct by luxury car drivers (Huang et al., 2020). While these cases may shine light on those in positions of power, these practices are more likely to impact the lives of civilians who lack capital and privilege. Both press and scholars may rely on the term 'citizen' to describe these individuals (cf. Rosie et al., 2006), yet this term reinforces the exclusion of non-citizens in many forms of mediated scrutiny and shaming. Discourse about concerned individuals is often tied up with notions of citizenry, which is meant to provide a unified bond, emphasising a status as 'normal' people. 'Normal' can be interpreted as humble, lacking additional resources or mandates compared to police and the state. However, it is also normative and exclusionary as it taps into a set of values, but also rights and privileges that migrants and unhoused communities in the same locale do not possess. While lacking legal privileges, non-citizens can participate through digital tools, hence our choice to use the term civilians to include them. Yet factors such as an undocumented status or reliance on a temporary visa remain vulnerabilities for these individuals.

We see a tension between global repertoires and local manifestations in empirical cases. Even globalised forms of outrage against a consensus immoral act like child sexual abuse are locally situated and made meaningful according to local circumstances. In Canada, *The Judge Beauce* is shown to mobilise different types of capital (Dupont, 2004), to sustain itself and successfully catch and shame suspected pedophiles. These efforts came under criticism for using a visual identity that resembles local biker gangs (Myles & Trottier, 2017). In seeking economic capital through merchandise and social capital through their recognisability, their visual association with prominent local crime organisations harms their cultural capital, and consequently their political capital. In China, concerned civilians form networks and use Sina Weibo to expose pedophiles. These civilians do not necessarily have hacking or computational knowledge. The most common tactic they use is going undercover into pedophile networks in the form of Sina Weibo Circles and

QQ/WeChat groups, which are mostly established for selling and distributing child pornography.[8] After collecting sufficient evidence, civilians with technological knowledge then publish the personal information of the distributors and group members on social media platforms. In these public posts, concerned individuals also tag local police accounts and state media to augment the visibility of – and thus public attention on – their cases, increasing pressure on local police to take action. Meanwhile, anti-pedophile netizens avoid any criticism or negative attitudes towards police in these posts, as it is understood in China that criticism of the government may be regarded as a potential threat to social stability and will lead to censorship or other interventions. The lack of criticism does not mean that these participants fully trust local authorities as they choose to report the cases publicly on social media instead of only reporting directly to local police. Often, cases that are only reported directly to local police may be disregarded if they are not considered urgent. The manner that concerned civilians in China strategically navigate the local police's boundaries demonstrates unique local dynamics.

In Russia, pedophile hunting activities were popularised by a neo-Nazi group *Restruct* under the leadership of Maxim Martsinkevich, widely known by his nickname *Tesak* [Hatchet]. Vigilantes would punish and humiliate their targets by beating them, shaving off their hair and forcing them to drink urine. Targets were obliged to display their legal IDs to the camera and sometimes would have to call their relatives or employers and reveal themselves as pedophiles (Favarel-Garrigues & Gayer,2024). This retaliation process known as 'safaris' would be filmed and shared across social media platforms, gaining millions of views and international popularity. Through such activities, neo-Nazis in Russia became "moral entrepreneurs" as they generated income through the monetisation of their social media accounts (Favarel-Garrigues 2020, p. 306). Alleged pedophiles targeted by *Restruct* were often teenage sexual minorities. Given the wider homophobic atmosphere in Russia and respective legislation on banning 'gay propaganda,'[9] targets can hardly count on any path to legal justice. A respondent working on issues of nationalism in Russia states the following:

> Police were often going on raids along with the vigilantes. In smaller towns, the situation was the worst as you could never say anything [after you have been humiliated]. If they found out that you went to the police, they could beat you again, or even kill you.

Tesak, as the mastermind behind the popularisation of denunciation via social media, became a saintlike figure for Russia's neo-Nazis. He started a few other formations, targeting drug dealers and illegal migrants. Nevertheless, wide publicity did not grant Tesak any immunity as the state eventually came after him. The state realised the potential harm that a neo-Nazi formation could bring to its public image as well as to regime security. After a series of convictions, in 2020 Tesak mysteriously died in prison at the age of thirty-six.[10] Authorities ruled suicide as the cause of death – which was contested by Tesak's lawyer and supporters. According to the respondent above, some followers still seek guidance in their vigilant endeavours by asking the rhetorical question "What would Tesak do?"

Concerned individuals also target plagiarism on a global scale. Across countries, writers watch over other writers in professional associations and networks, including academics, journalists, essayists and fiction authors. Consider the US-based *Retraction Watch*, a blog that reports scholarly publications being retracted "as a window into the scientific process."[11] While focusing on a broader range of academic misconduct, plagiarism features prominently in its blog posts featuring English-language instances in locations like Poland, Mexico and Pakistan. This scrutiny and shaming also targets prominent figures, in part because they are the public face of their profession and are seen as reflecting its wider reputation. More prominent cases can also risk slipping into greater media spectacles seen in Chapter 3. In China, denouncing plagiarism has been routinised in the forms of dedicated public accounts on WeChat, Sina Weibo or Red that expose scholars, artists and designers who poached the works of others. Some of the cases exposed on these accounts may generate a larger scale of public discussion or formal investigations, such as when a Chinese Academy of Arts professor was denounced and fired for plagiarising London-based artist Seana Gavin.[12] Yet most cases remain visible within the communities formed surrounding these accounts. In Russia, "a free online community"[13] of journalists and academics called *Dissernet* engage in scrutiny and exposure of unscrupulous scholars, including falsified and otherwise fraudulent PhD defences. Relying on plagiarism detection software, *Dissernet* community members track similarities in academic articles and PhD dissertations and expose their targets online. Prominent academics and politicians are common figures in these investigations. As of February 2024, *Dissernet* exposed nearly nine thousand individuals on their website.[14] The community filed nearly two thousand complaints with Russia's high examination committee, and over one thousand PhD degrees have been revoked. While members of the high examination committee and other high-profile individuals in Russia are exposed on *Dissernet*, for the most part, they appear to be immune when it comes to losing their degrees. *Dissernet* has also grown beyond Russia's borders and is now active in thirty-five countries.

The people denouncing plagiarism are not simply civilians or amateurs, but are in some way financially or professionally invested in a job sector. This personal involvement in their field motivates them to watch over threats to their economic and professional well-being. Such self-preservation by scrutiny and reporting of others is a common feature in any community (Madsen, 2004). This ubiquity is further assisted by the uptake of digital tools, which can both enhance geographic proximity as well as overcome its absence. Even when these tools are restricted to localised social networks, users can leak digital fragments such as screenshots or emails, which has become a global media practice (Corry, 2021).

User perspectives: initial reactions and justifications to participate

While mediated denunciation is longstanding, contemporary digital practices compel people to reflect on how they can intervene in the lives of others, or at least make their misdeeds visible. This often involves making sense of being on the other end of the process: how individuals are coming to terms with being scrutinised and targeted by others. Sensemaking is an ongoing process, not only because platforms and hardware are subject to revisions and upgrades, but because these are further embedded in diverse social contexts, often provoking disagreement and hostility from others. This partly explains why social media users collectively and perpetually situate themselves in the infancy stage of its usage (cf. Trottier 2012). Even if someone has used Facebook for nearly two decades, perpetual changes to the platform and its user base may contribute to a perceived uncertainty about how the site will be used in the future.

The justifications people provide for watching over others explain specific incidents, but also broader shaming practices they anticipate enacting in the future. For some respondents, the motives are obvious, and are meant to be obvious to those who share a broadly compatible world view. The offences themselves include alarming concerns, such as self-avowed Nazis marching in public. An American data scientist and activist cites the gravity of local far-right extremism as a factor for her work: "And certainly afterwards we knew that it was going to be a focal point for many years to come. So it started with trying to understand, OK, who are these people that are coming right? Who are these neo-Nazis?" Even legal professionals may support mediated denunciation for incidents that are not punishable by law yet carry a negative impact on social morality. A Chinese law professor expressed his anger about an incident involving a woman who was accused of causing her friend's death and lying about it afterwards,[15] and justified the online shaming against her:

> I don't normally support punishment without legal due process. However, cases like this are special because they can't really be punished by law. How can you punish someone for lying and being immoral? But if [her] behaviour goes unpunished, what kind of message are we sending society?

Respondents also point to lesser issues that are nevertheless unjustifiable, such as discarded dog feces on public walkways. A UK-based community leader addressed above mentions the persistence of dog feces in local public spaces as grounds for an initiative to combat this nuisance: "people were complaining about the state of the village because children were walking to school and they got mess on their shoes. (…) [I]t's just been a very nasty situation. So people wanted to put a stop to it." In terms of inactivity from local authorities, she adds that this issue "had been an agenda item on the parish council agenda for six years" and that it "hadn't been tackled." These responses locate an external harm as the starting point to mediated denunciation, as opposed to technological possibilities or personal dispositions. Some participants also justify their involvement based on the skills they possess to gather data on these offences, recognising that other implicated members of a local community may be unable to do this.

The turn to digital engagement is presented as necessary when defusing a situation in person is not plausible. A UK-based journalist reflects on her own experience being targeted by someone attempting to denounce her on a Facebook group. Following a hostile exchange on public transit, she acknowledges that diffusing such situations in person is rare, and that she should not have bothered: "the more I think about it, it's very rare that you speak to someone in person really angry and they get less angry. Like, they tend to wind themselves up more." While public discourse laments a loss of face-to-face resolutions in the era of social media,[16] her ordeal speaks to how hostile exchanges on a train or other public settings may not be easily defused (cf. Trottier et al., 2020).

Local terrains as regional and professional proximity

Those engaged in online denunciation make sense of these experiences through their involvement in a local terrain. In these cases, being located in a specific environment involves a kind of dependency and commitment that is cause for mobilisation. Being local is understood as being in touch with people who are aware of their immediate environment, whether in a regional or professional sense. Our respondents also make use of digital tools that transcend local contexts to combat social problems that also transcend local contexts. Thus, concerned individuals may work with diverse types of supporting connections. Some may be proximate and sustained, while others are temporary yet vital, notably in providing legitimating evidence in a mediated denunciation of someone. The data scientist above describes these links in the context of her own actions:

> I post something on Twitter, somebody else takes it and they try to call that guy's mom or that guy's employer. Right. So if I'm going to drop a dime on Twitter like that, I'm going to bring receipts because (…) I want to get all the evidence so that if anyone decides to do this, they can also protect themselves. And it lends credibility, like, 'yeah, we found this guy. We know that he's doing X, Y, Z. Here's the evidence of it. Here's how we

> know it's him,' you know, not saying go do something about it. I'm just saying be aware of it.

This respondent adds that above all else her objective is to make others aware of threatening or hostile people in their own local environments. The goal "typically is not to harass or intimidate or threaten" but rather to "make people aware in their communities that they have potentially violent and bigoted people in their midst." This awareness suggests a pervasive media engagement that seeks to mobilise an entire community.

It also matters who the local public actually is. When the UK-based journalist discovered she was denounced on an Australian Facebook page, the lack of proximity was reason to not be vigilant about its spread:

> I was like, I'm not going to come into contact with this naturally. (…) So I felt like my need to police it just felt quite minimal. If he'd posted on some kind of [local area] group where, like, someone I worked with might see it, I probably would have gotten comfortable, like trying to find it and reporting it.

A central dimension of concern in the 'local' is the vulnerabilities associated with the knowledge of one's location. Here local is often a fixed location where others can bring harm to an individual. A Dutch knowledge worker recounts her experiences with her personal and professional information being published on *Dumpert*, a prominent Dutch media-hosting site. She expresses concern that participants on this website could have come to her door, noting that it is difficult to ensure that this did not already happen:

> they could have gotten to our doors. Maybe people they had done that, you know, like, go over to our house and actually you know, that this happens with people who are suspects from sex offenses, for example (…) or the Eindhoven *Kopschoppers* [head kickers].[17] People were actually going to houses. So (…) the consequences can become very embodied.

She not only situates the possibility of front door interventions based on more general categories like sex offenders, but also local high-profile cases that featured prominently in Dutch media. Interestingly, her case stems from a poster placed in her neighbourhood, that was photographed and eventually uploaded to *Dumpert*. Upon gaining large-scale visibility on national media, the outcome was a threat at the local and embodied level at which her ordeal began. Context shapes how personal content is received by a given public. What is appropriate in a local setting in terms of public conduct or expression can be reframed negatively elsewhere. Local contexts and conditions are reasons for concerned individuals to mobilise, and sources of vulnerability that may lead to denunciation and crowdsourced targeting from hostile actors.

Political polarisation as a global accelerant of vigilantism and shaming

Political and cultural polarisation involving media and public figures is a frequent and prominent dimension in the context in which concerned individuals watch over others. It appears to fuel many cases, even when the case is ostensibly about something else. Given the prevailing intolerance of child sexual abuse, terms like 'groomer' or 'pedophile' are frequently leveraged against political opponents.[18] And in the context of the COVID-19 pandemic, wearing a face mask almost immediately expanded from a minor public health measure in order to map onto political fault lines in countries like the US and the Netherlands (Lang et al., 2021; Keijzer & Mepham, 2021).

People may be driven by a need to stop social harms, and in feeling compelled they also make assumptions about the targeted person that connects them to a broader profile of the kinds of people concerned individuals are mobilised against, including pedophiles, Nazis and elites. Respondents point to elections as evidence of recent change. A Dutch knowledge worker highlights political debates as a site of degradation, noting that: "the tone of voice has changed how people how politicians treat one another, talk about each other (…) I see a shift towards more disrespectful language." An American essayist highlights the post-Trump era and Trump's media savvy as pivotal in shaping public discourse:

> [E]verything becomes a spectacle (…) I do see Trump as an extremely formidable opponent. (…) He's a smart guy who knows how to divide, manipulate. All these things that he learned from thirty… I don't know, like all of the years in *The Apprentice* and in reality TV.

Scaling up his focus, this respondent comments on the broader media environment in which such tactics seem to flourish:

> We're in an attention economy where, like, [Trump] knows how to bring one thing to get people's attention, distract them from other things he's trying to do or policy he's trying to push that doesn't get coverage at all just by saying something completely outrageous.

This reference to an "attention economy" suggests the emergence of business and campaign models based engaging users through provocative content, and is further discussed in Chapter 4. Not only are alt-right media figures adopting such tactics (Korostelina, 2016), but respondents treat the emergence of seemingly emboldened Nazis as cause for heightened vigilance.

Facing political polarisation on a global scale, some respondents note that intent matters when distinguishing acceptable from unacceptable forms of online denunciation. Technical skills, practices and terminology may transcend political ideologies, so these respondents suggest that a part of whether they are deemed acceptable should be who is denouncing, and for what reasons. In this book we discuss ideologically diverse cases that make up a broader set of practices while distinguishing between causes we support and those we condemn. A common feature is that digital media visibility is more likely to be localised in polarised as well as performative spaces, where changes of opinion and dispute resolution fall from the spotlight. A Canadian journalist notes that such moments do occur online, albeit in less visible corners:

> I see it a lot in direct messages, especially when there's not that public pressure to over perform your point and to be able to show a bit of vulnerability and to be able to, you know, really acknowledge, I guess, the other position that the person that you're debating or that you're discussing with may have.

Bilateral resolutions of grievances are seemingly possible on digital platforms. They may bring a more positive outcome, compared to the disproportionate spectacle targets endure. Yet this requires a vulnerability that appears incompatible with how concerned individuals use Twitter threads and other public fora.

Risk of job loss, but not from tourists?

Seeing these events unfold ends up informing respondents' understandings of conditions of visibility. Beyond outcomes in exceptional events, they cultivate an understanding of what it means to be visible online. In terms of making sense of watching and being watched, we recognise these as expectations and guidelines that allow participants to make sense of individual cases, but also with the possibility that this can generalise to a more enduring state of what it means to be visible on the internet. Most of our respondents would not be considered public figures, but still have some experience with being watched and watching online. In some cases this may be due to a sustained submission of personal or professional content as an author or podcaster. Other respondents may abstain from the internet, but a moment of exposure then leads to an ordeal that in turn shapes their opinions, beliefs and fears.

After her experiences with online exposure, a Dutch filmmaker is acutely aware of and concerned about cameras in public. Yet she also distinguishes between camera-wielding locals and tourists. Much like the UK-based journalist above, she regards foreign individuals bearing cameras as less of a threat: "I'm so aware of all the cameras, all the cameras people have, it makes me afraid as well. And sometimes I need to tell myself, don't be afraid (…) because it's not like you're ending up on *Dumpert*. Those are tourists." Those who are public-facing have general exposure on platforms, and often face harms that come from visibility, such as harassment and counter-denunciation. These harms may stem from categorical discrimination on the basis of gender, ethnicity, sexual orientation, as well as ideological grounds when profiled as a 'left-wing elitist.' A concern here is that very little information about the target themselves is necessary to 'fill the blanks' in order to make a public judgment about the type of person they are. In terms of harassment and harm, the Dutch filmmaker expresses an ambivalence corresponding to what they consider to be the two sides of the internet: bullying and responses to bullying, or in other words harm and retributive justice. The internet allows for people to harm and harass others, but also allows others to sanction those deemed responsible for these harms. In turn, such justice-seeking may become excessive or disproportionate. The contemporary digital media landscape can deliver something proximate to social justice, which she describes as "a really good weapon to get somebody punished."

A common theme across our interviews is the extent to which people's jobs are targeted in practice. We may interpret employment as a kind of low hanging fruit because, according to the Canadian journalist jobs are "proven to be vulnerable." This statement acknowledges a larger scale socio-economic condition: precarity and vulnerability on the job market as a wide-reaching condition that has a direct impact on nearly anybody's personal well-being. A viral misstep can disrupt someone's ability to pay their bills and feed their family. This vulnerability impacts people to varying degrees, as some are able to rely on personal savings or a wealthy family. Yet job loss remains a widely persistent threat.

Another tension is apparent: mediated visibility makes people seen and heard, but also serves to dehumanise them. The American essayist describes this as a process where identified people become a punching bag, adding that he "just do[es]n't have that much faith for the Internet's ability to kind of mature in that way." He also adds that "social media platforms like Twitter don't have the interest for that either" as toxic people drive further engagement on platforms. In terms of asymmetrical forms of visibility, where less visible people attack a highly visible target, some public sentiment favours curbing anonymity by making real names visible in order to post on social media.[19] We may question whether such initiatives can dampen online abuse, and consider the role of platforms in mediated shaming more generally in Chapter 4.

Lessons learned about digital harms

Following their experiences with online scrutiny, participants refer to the insights they gained. Some are practical, like being more hesitant to film others in public. The UK-based journalist notes:

> I haven't done it since that event because I was like, even if I'm just sharing it with one person, it's still like taking an image of someone outside of their control. And also I was like, if they caught me doing it, I wouldn't have a good explanation for why I'm doing it. It would just be like 'I'm sending my sister a picture of you and your dogs.' Like it's not… if it's hard to explain and you're only doing it for a really quick response. It's kind of… yeah. So I've definitely stopped.

As a practice, taking photos of strangers in public is an important source of user-generated content on digital platforms, but also a potential harm to others that in turn is difficult to explain or justify. She proposes instead to provide a written description of something she may otherwise decide to photograph, noting that this would anonymise the person being targeted. Some respondents state that concerned individuals need to focus on their role in this process, in contrast to a discourse that focuses on an online mob. Even when shared with a closed group, there remains a persistent risk that digital media may leak to a wider audience.

In addition to tactics to minimise harm to others, digital media users clearly develop strategies to prevent reputational harm to themselves, namely through practices related to digital platforms. Many Chinese citizens are closely familiar with storing 'evidence' to counter potential denunciations against them. Some people also take advantage of platform affordances. After experiencing three rounds of public shaming, a Chinese content creator configured her Sina Weibo posts to "only content from the past three months are visible, so that people can't dig what I said back then and take them out of context to attack me." Some participants also distinguish themselves as being well suited for turbulent mediated exposure. In contrast, we may consider the welfare and struggles of those who do not have the constitution to endure being public-facing. At an individual level we can consider predispositions like having 'thick skin.' The Canadian journalist refers to herself as an "open book," adding that she has been online for a long time. Yet she does not think being open is good for her career and would not encourage those who are shy to put themselves in an uncomfortable position online:

> You know, it's like when you decided to already be an open book online, then you kind of just have to lean into it. And if someone decides that they don't want to be an open book online, then you have to really take other precautions or be careful in other ways. Like a lot of people obviously have anonymous accounts, which is a way to be able to express yourself and not, you know, [deal with] fear, reprisal or whatever.

The perceived pressure to be an 'open book' in some capacity online may be felt by those on the job market or in search of clients, patronage or support, especially among those working in the media sector. We can speculate that those who would describe themselves as having thick skin are more likely to express contentious views online. They are likely also more willing to speak about such incidents, including in the interviews we conducted. These individual differences matter because they suggest diverging experiences of online shaming that may not fit with our findings, in part due to self-selection among those who engage and actively respond to online shaming. Some respondents dislike being visible, especially when their most prominent exposure is involuntary. The Dutch knowledge worker avoids being photographed or recorded but also acknowledges its importance, and struggles with this demand to some degree: "I also know that from training that it's important to brand yourself and to make your work more visible." Here the fact that these demands come from career training suggests ongoing professional responses to mediated visibility are a topic that should be further explored.

Stepping away from individual traits, it bears noting that exposure to online scrutiny is not simply a personal choice but also shaped by one's social identity. Some may have the disposition, privilege or capital to take on these struggles. Others do not have the option to decide and are instead thrown into the digital fray. We can question if pressure to be visible online may steer some job candidates away from sectors like media or civil service, especially if they belong to marginalised communities or see themselves as vulnerable in some other way.

Reflecting on long-term harms and opportunities

Reporting on the court of public opinion is often centred on the moment of denunciation, in other words, the exposition and viral spike in attention. Yet there is an aftermath that may not provoke as much concern or awareness among those who participate in denunciations. We may inquire about a longer-lasting impact on those who are targeted by online denunciation, and whether a proportionate response is attainable in mediated shaming. Some respondents note the potential for totalising punishment as the most damaging way to harm people. The Dutch knowledge worker hopes that people are not aware of the social, reputational and psychological harms they are doing, as knowingly committing to such harms are an even more troubling prospect:

> I don't think that they realize what... what they do to people, I don't think they realize that. Or actually I hope they don't realize it because otherwise it would be really disturbing that they would harm people with intent, on purpose. And maybe that's the case even, that they don't care.

Yet these harms are not easy to avoid when looking at instances where there is an excess of vitriol. Those who engage in denunciation may have troubled relationships with their own decisions, even if ultimately supporting them. The American essayist states that he is not a fan of vigilantism due to the loss of nuance in public discourse. He recognises its usefulness given the violation of professional norms with plagiarism, yet he would normally wish to confront the offender at an earlier and less visible moment.

Participants are also ambivalent about boundaries of what is actionable more generally. A media designer based in the Netherlands laments the hard-line pursuit of targets and an absence of forgiveness in public fora, yet also understands why some denunciations need to take a more extremist stance:

> There's no forgiveness on the internet, in these cases of digital vigilantism. And for sure, it's a bad thing. But I kind of understand that in the beginning it needs to be sometimes very extremist [in] approaches to stuff. And as the same happened, maybe with feminism in the beginning, where it's very extremist, the movements try to impose some change that then it will be more balanced.

In terms of specific cases, the American essayist describes the #MeToo movement from a comparable lens. While it is inherently good, he believes there is a lack of balancing mechanisms: "I mean, all of it is, you know, inherently good trying to pursue justice. But I don't think they do have the safeguards on it to have that kind of debate after or even nuance." Ultimately, the social benefits brought by these public denunciations "outweigh any of the harm done, you know, unless I mean, except for the most extreme cases." He goes on to distinguish denunciatory practices from a formal court:

> This isn't a court, you know, and I know a lot of people have been disappointed by actions, or like, inaction rather than within the courts. But in here you still have some of the same implications of a court, you know, but in a way that's very difficult to describe.

Likewise, the Canadian journalist understands these assessments as a ubiquitous condition that is rooted in, but also transcends local context, such that "it also takes people beyond their social circles or geographic location to build that profile." Yet in practice legal and ethical dimensions quickly become too much of a burden to effectively handle, leading to denunciation and shaming responses that are not proportionate to the sense of injustice or collective reproach.

In terms of broader trajectories, the Dutch filmmaker claims we still do not know the long-term consequences of being denounced, as well as being involved in a media environment where one denounces others: "I think now we have a lot of cases that have happened now and in the last year. So we don't know the consequences when this girl wants to get a job or find somebody she wants to marry, and the [incriminating] video pops up." In the Chinese fandom incident mentioned above, a Xiao Zhan fan highlighted the emotional burden brought by the undesired visibility:

> I still cry everyday since then [three months ago]. I don't think I'm depressed, but I feel so much anger and, you know, different kinds of negative emotions whenever I think about how we [as a fan community] got all the hate. They [The 227 United] are doing exactly what they are opposing.

While some respondents like the American essayist see that the personal impact of denunciation and shaming "almost goes away" with time, this is from the vantage point of a person who engaged in public denunciation, rather than being targeted by it.

Conclusion

This chapter focuses on people engaged in the sensemaking of watching and being watched, as well as denouncing and being denounced. People feel compelled to participate in scrutiny because they are aware of ongoing threats that range from fascists to dog feces. This often involves watching over and preserving a local territory, or helping others do the same. Yet the local space is not just something that makes these struggles meaningful, but also invokes its own vulnerabilities. Content from this local context can be extracted and reinterpreted in an uncharitable manner. Likewise, hostile actors can enter the locale, for instance when showing up at a target's front door.[20] For better and worse, digitally mediated shaming operates through a reproduction of local knowledge and repertoires. A key takeaway is that online environments should not be understood in contrast to offline ones. Rather, Facebook pages and other online spaces are both localised and leaky. While they are fuelled and made meaningful through local concerns, they easily exceed these boundaries. In going beyond local contexts, some individuals may accrue heightened visibility through a high follower count and temporary fame or notoriety. Their public shaming is often reported as celebrity gossip (Hirdman, 2017), tabloid content (Milbrandt, 2017) or social commentary (Jorge et al., 2021). The next chapter addresses this more spectacular side of the court of public opinion.

Our respondents also recommend that digital media users cultivate empathy for those on the other side of the screen. This includes being curious about what drives others to plagiarise or engage in other misdeeds. To be clear, this is a burdensome task when it comes to self-avowed Nazis or people accused of child sexual abuse. Yet awareness-raising campaigns for a general public and targeted educational material can compel digital media users to take a more restrained and measured approach when taking offence online.[21]

Notes

1 https://www.sixthtone.com/news/1005286
2 https://twitter.com/Pretpark020
3 https://www.instagram.com/pdx.real/
4 https://www.thepaper.cn/newsDetail_forward_1490897
5 https://www.mic.com/culture/why-is-lockheed-martin-the-twitter-person-of-the-day
6 https://www.wabp.nl/
7 https://www.wabp.nl/voor-wie/politie/
8 http://www.xinhuanet.com/english/2018-02/07/c_136956805.htm
9 What started as a ban on "gay propaganda" in 2013 intensified over the years and in 2023 culminated in the Supreme Court's ruling that deemed the "international LGBT movement" an extremist organisation (https://www.hrw.org/news/2024/02/15/russia-first-convictions-under-lgbt-extremist-ruling). It is important to note that there is no such registered legal entity, thus anyone deviating from the official view of traditional sexuality may be deemed an extremist.
10 https://www.rferl.org/a/russia-martsenkevich-antigay-ultranationalis-suicide-note/30983722.html
11 https://retractionwatch.com/
12 https://www.sixthtone.com/news/1012807
13 https://www.dissernet.org/about
14 https://www.dissernet.org/person
15 https://www.sixthtone.com/news/1001175
16 https://medium.com/@danthecoach/why-you-must-always-confront-haters-face-to-face-e66d814489b9
17 A prominent Dutch digital vigilantism incident from 2013, see https://socialmedia-dna.nl/kopschoppers/
18 https://www.vox.com/culture/23025505/leftist-groomers-homophobia-satanic-panic-explained
19 See for example: https://petition.parliament.uk/petitions/575833
20 https://www.mareonline.nl/achtergrond/het-was-zo-eng-ik-stond-te-shaken-op-mijn-benen/
21 See for example: https://sire.nl/campagnes/doeslief/

References

Andersson Schwarz, J. (2017). Platform logic: An interdisciplinary approach to the platform-based economy. *Policy & Internet*, *9*(4), 374–394. https://doi.org/10.1002/poi3.159

Corry, F. (2021). Screenshot, save, share, shame: Making sense of new media through screenshots and public shame. *First Monday*, *26*(4–5). https://doi.org/10.5210/fm.v26i4.11649

Dobash, R. P., & Dobash, R. E. (1981). Community response to violence against wives: Charivari, abstract justice and patriarchy. *Social Problems*, *28*(5), 563–581. https://doi.org/10.2307/800231

Douglas, D. M. (2020). Doxing as audience vigilantism against hate speech. In D. Trottier, R. Gabdulhakov, & Q. Huang (Eds.),*Introducing vigilant audiences* (pp. 259–279). Open Book Publishers. https://doi.org/10.11647/obp.0200.10

Dupont, B. (2004). Security in the age of networks. *Policing and Society*, *14*(1), 76–91. https://doi.org/10.1080/1043946042000181575

Favarel-Garrigues, G. (2020). Digital vigilantism and anti-paedophile activism in Russia. Between civic involvement in law enforcement, moral policing and business venture. *Global Crime*, *21*(3–4), 306–326. https://doi.org/10.1080/17440572.2019.1676738

Favarel-Garrigues, G., & Gayer, L. (2024). *Proud to punish: The global landscapes of rough justice*. Stanford University Press. https://doi.org/10.1515/9781503637689

Gabdulhakov, R. (2018). Citizen-led justice in post-communist Russia: From comrades' courts to dotcomrade vigilantism. *Surveillance & Society*, *16*(3), 314–331. https://doi.org/10.24908/ss.v16i3.6952

Gabdulhakov, R. (2019). In the bullseye of vigilantes: Mediated vulnerabilities of Kyrgyz labour migrants in Russia. *Media and Communication, 7*(2), 230–241. https://doi.org/10.17645/mac.v7i2.1927

Gorman, P. (2017) Red guard 2.0: Nationalist flesh search in China. *Journal of Contemporary China*, *26*(104), 183–198. https://doi.org/10.1080/10670564.2016.1223102

Haggerty, K. D., & Ericson, R. V. (2000). The surveillant assemblage. *British Journal of Sociology*, *51*(4), 605–622. https://doi.org/10.1080/00071310020015280

Hintz, A., Dencik, L., & Wahl-Jorgensen, K. (2017). Digital citizenship and surveillance| digital citizenship and surveillance society—introduction. *International Journal of Communication*, *11*, 9. https://ijoc.org/index.php/ijoc/article/view/5521/1929

Hirdman, A. (2017). Flesh-images, body shame and affective ambiguities in celebrity gossip magazines. *Celebrity Studies*, *8*(3), 365–377. https://doi.org/10.1080/19392397.2017.1283244

Huang, Q., Gabdulhakov, R., & Trottier, D. (2020). Online scrutiny of people with nice cars: A comparative analysis of Chinese, Russian, and Anglo-American outrage. *Global Media and China*, *5*(3), 247–260. https://doi.org/10.1177/2059436420901818

Huang, Q., Driessen, S., & Trottier, D. (2023). When pop and politics collide: A transcultural perspective on contested practices in pop idol fandoms in China and the West. *International Journal of Communication*, *17*, 1425–1444. https://ijoc.org/index.php/ijoc/article/view/17255

Jorge, A., Oliva, M., & Aguiar, L. L. (2021). Offshoring & leaking: Cristiano Ronaldo's tax evasion, and celebrity in neoliberal times. *Popular Communication*, *19*(3), 178–192. https://doi.org/10.1080/15405702.2021.1913491

Keijzer, M. A., & Mepham, K. D. (2021). Een pandemie van polarisatie? *Mens & Maatschappij*, *96*(2), 179–211. https://doi.org/10.5117/mem2021.2.003.keij

Korostelina, K. V. (2016). *Trump effect.* Taylor & Francis. https://doi.org/10.4324/9781315271170

Kucherov, Samuel. 1970. *The organs of soviet administration of justice: Their history and operation.* Brill.

Kudaibergenova, D. T. (2020). The body global and the body traditional: A digital ethnography of Instagram and nationalism in Kazakhstan and Russia. In J. Beyer & P. Finke (Eds.), *Practices of traditionalization in central Asia* (pp. 54–71). Routledge. https://doi.org/10.4324/9781003018964-4

Lang, J., Erickson, W. W., & Jing-Schmidt, Z. (2021). #MaskOn! #MaskOff! Digital polarization of mask-wearing in the United States during COVID-19.*PloS One*, *16*(4), e0250817. https://doi.org/10.1371/journal.pone.0250817

Louis, M. R. (1980). Surprise and sense making: What newcomers experience in entering unfamiliar organizational settings. *Administrative Science Quarterly*, *25*(2), 226–251.

Madsen, M. L. (2004). Living for home: Policing immorality among undocumented migrants in Johannesburg. *African Studies*, *63*(2), 173–192. https://doi.org/10.1080/00020180412331318742

Marwick, A. (2012). The public domain: Surveillance in everyday life. *Surveillance & Society*, *9*(4), 378–393. https://doi.org/10.24908/ss.v9i4.4342

Moores, C. (2017). Thatcher's troops? Neighbourhood watch schemes and the search for 'ordinary' Thatcherism in 1980s Britain. *Contemporary British History*, *31*(2), 230–255. https://doi.org/10.1080/13619462.2017.1306203

Milbrandt, T. (2017). Caught on camera, posted online: Mediated moralities, visual politics and the case of urban 'drought-shaming'.*Visual Studies*, *32*(1), 3–23. https://doi.org/10.1080/1472586x.2016.1246952

Myles, D., & Trottier, D. (2017). Leveraging visibility, gaining capital? Social media use in the fight against child abusers: The case of the judge Beauce. *Social Media + Society*, *3*(1). https://doi.org/10.1177/2056305117691998

Rosie, M., Petersoo, P., MacInnes, J., Condor, S., & Kennedy, J. (2006). Mediating which nation? Citizenship and national identities in the British press. *Social Semiotics*, *16*(2), 327–344. https://doi.org/10.1080/10350330600664896

Solove, D. J. (2007).*The future of reputation: Gossip, rumor, and privacy on the internet.* Yale University Press. https://doi.org/10.12987/9780300138191

Trottier, D. (2012). *Social media as surveillance: Rethinking visibility in a converging world.* Ashgate. https://doi.org/10.4324/9781315609508

Trottier, D., Huang, Q., & Gabdulhakov, R. (2020). Mediated visibility as making vitriol meaningful. In S. Polak & D. Trottier (Eds.), *Violence and trolling on social media* (pp. 25–46). Amsterdam University Press. https://doi.org/10.1515/9789048542048-003

3 Prominent users

(Micro-)celebrity and cancellation

cancel.influenceurs as bilateral denunciation of prominent figures

During the second wave of the COVID-19 pandemic, local authorities urged the public to limit non-essential travel. Politicians, royal families and influencers who gained prominence on platforms like Instagram continued to go on holidays. In the Canadian province of Québec, many influencers posted content about beach parties and airport lounges on their accounts, to their many followers. These images led to denunciation across digital media, including on an Instagram page entitled *cancel.influenceurs*.[1] This page reposts images and videos of prominent influencers travelling to warmer locations like Miami and the Caribbean. Members also source screenshots from influencers' temporary stories that would otherwise be deleted. The nature of these denunciations is remarkable as they received scorn from both socially progressive[2] and regressive[3] local online venues. In a rare development, polarised digital communities were temporarily aligned in their hostility towards influencers flaunting public health guidelines. In most instances, we not only find disagreement about who should be the target of public denunciation but also about whether 'cancel culture' itself exists as something more than a talking point.[4]

Influencers' vulnerability to such denunciation is due to the visibility of the antisocial behaviour that they record and publish. It is also a product of their status as influencers, as they build a substantial audience through followers and viral distribution beyond their accounts. Their designation as influencers suggests being public-facing, and thus fair game for scrutiny and denunciation. In the context of *cancel.influenceurs*, cancellation suggests an attempt to terminate – or at least tarnish – that status. As discussed in Chapter 1, cancellation is framed in public discourse as both a process of accountability and weaponised attack on an enemy or target. This aligns with the moral ambivalence of other media practices such as doxing, digital vigilantism and denunciation more generally. The practice of calling attention to misdeeds extends to other offences on *cancel.influenceurs*, as footage of blackface and sexist behaviour also ends up on a page that was initially designated for covid-shaming. From a social justice perspective, one can witness countless harms

DOI: 10.4324/9781003453017-3

online that warrant a response. From a digital media studies perspective, platforms like Twitter and Instagram become venues for monitoring and denunciation. Cancellation of prominent public figures is one of the most tangible verdicts of public opinion, and forces media audiences to come to terms with the existence and possible expansion of the court of public opinion. It is tangible in the sense that we devote so much media attention to explicitly addressing it as a practice. In other cases, public discourse may simply focus on the target and offence they committed, without also explicitly using a term like cancellation to capture how audiences and other media actors have retaliated. At the same time, we are witnessing the spread of cancel culture discourse and practice to targets who cannot be considered prominent, but may still be public-facing, including educators[5] and small business owners.[6]

This chapter addresses prominent visibility as a condition for influencers and other public figures, but also as indicative of emerging conditions for those with a lesser online following. Shaming incidents often take place under the banner of cancel culture. The term 'cancel culture' is a placeholder for earlier conversations about political correctness,[7] but also speaks to the dynamics of contemporary mediated visibility that transcend ideology and national borders. Across media environments, being made visible in a negative way can bring profound and persistent harm. We are concerned with both the so-called 'culture wars' linked to political polarisation (Sobolewska & Ford, 2020), and a more generalised struggle to be visible in public. Prominent individuals like influencers can mobilise a greater following against targets, whether those targets are fellow influencers or 'ordinary' people. Yet as we see, this increased prominence is also a vulnerability for them, and backlash against their viral prominence seems inevitable.

We are witnessing a mainstreaming of 'extremely online'[8] culture, as online exchanges – including trolling (Phillips, 2015), harassment (Paasonen et al., 2019) and calls for accountability (Nakamura, 2015) – are growing concerns for individuals and organisations. 'Online' is at times denigrated as something neither serious nor real. Online exchanges are framed as not only noxious but also frivolous and easily avoided by spending less time on our devices. Terms like "doom scrolling"[9] and "irony poisoning"[10] present toxic Twitter threads as bearing the same public health concern as alcohol or processed sugars. When "someone is wrong on the internet,"[11] a popular recommendation is to just "log off" and "touch grass"[12] rather than engage with antagonists.

Yet 'online' is often the sole infrastructure for social contact, composed of fora where people make sense of rapidly changing social conditions in the context of public health crises, but also the job market, the housing market, entertainment and politics. Consequently, more professional sectors are facing calls to communicate with the public via social media, including academic research (Heemstra, 2020). During the pandemic, nearly all facets of social and professional life were expected to fully migrate to online environments, such that being sat in front of a screen and keyboard became a full-time requirement. Still, the 'extremely online' refers to a subset of internet users who invest excessive time, get excessively emotionally invested in online affairs and have an excessive knowledge of fleeting incidents and cultural references. Some individuals are clearly more engaged than others, and there are many ways to measure engagement and differentiate users on these grounds. Yet those less engaged users are still living in an 'extremely online' culture, as they too can fall victim to – or otherwise get entangled in – online scrutiny and denunciation.

Online figures have long reckoned with positive and negative outcomes from their mediated visibility, including during the early days of personal blogging. In 2002, an American web designer was fired when her employer discovered that she was disparaging her co-workers on *Dooce*, her personal yet public blog that gained considerable recognition.[13] Her job loss was widely publicised, leading to debates about reasonable expectations of privacy in a digitised world. The term 'Dooced' emerged to describe the act of losing one's job because of something one posted online (Scaratti & Cortini, 2013). The public nature of her firing also drove traffic to her blog, as well as to other prominent content creators that made work of disparaging public figures.[14]

The people discussed in the previous chapter are also exposed to scrutiny, but to a lesser degree than those with higher follower counts and professional engagement in creative, cultural, political and other public-facing sectors. Below we consider individuals situated within an extremely online digital media landscape, based on their prominence. This chapter unpacks prominent users as a unifying concept. We explore conceptual dimensions of prominence to understand the challenges facing influencers, content creators and micro-celebrities (Marwick, 2013). This chapter is not an in-depth account of any single type of prominent media user. The focus is rather on the broader conditions of visibility via platforms, which make it possible to engage in scrutiny, shaming as well as degradation and disposal of individuals. The prominence we attribute to influencers and other public figures is implicitly and explicitly framed as success on platforms like TikTok (Abidin, 2021). Not only can one earn a living from their online visibility, but they exert greater socio-cultural clout through their ability to sustain and mobilise an online following. Yet this prominence also brings vulnerabilities, such as being cancelled due to the revelation of problematic and otherwise stigmatising personal details.

What does it mean to be prominent?

We can identify dimensions that distinguish prominent users from the individuals addressed in the previous chapter. First, there are several metrics on any given platform that help distinguish accounts that have a heightened social impact. This includes follower counts as well as several forms of engagement on posted content, such as 'likes,' 'replies' and 'reposts.' Certain types of status distinguish users, like being 'verified' on Twitter. Such measures can be made visible to any other user on the platform.[15] The user's professional designation may also contribute to being prominent, and often a public-facing profession such as a politician would go hand in hand with eventually being verified. Less tangibly, we can consider a digital media user's commitment to online discourse when employing particular terms, memes and ways of interpreting other users' activity (Daviess, 2019). This does not appear to be required for prominence, and in some public sectors may endanger one's authority, not only to a broader public but also in the eyes of one's own organisation (Rønn et al., 2024).

In theory and practice, prominence is multifaceted. Some of the above characteristics set a clear threshold where platforms and sponsors devote greater attention to one's profile and provide the user with more metrics about their content, for instance, to help make this content more "discoverable" to other users (McKelvey & Hunt, 2019, p. 4). Yet metrics like follower counts can be understood as a sliding scale, where a person with an order of magnitude more followers may not seem categorically different in terms of their prominence. Moreover, some digital media users lack a high follower count, yet identify with and strive towards this degree of prominence. Prominence is an attribute to describe anybody who develops enough attention and engagement on one or multiple platforms. They are a product of a longstanding rhetoric that frames users as empowered content creators,[16] but are distinguished in the degree of their success within an engagement economy.

Prominence is a unifying potential condition that is not exclusive to public figures. Rather, it is a potential for those who are public-facing, including through labour in the service sector. The journey from one hundred to one million followers is an uphill one, but seemingly without structural barriers. One can engage in the same kinds of practices they always do (producing content that provokes a reaction from their followers) and based on favourable conditions, someone may scale up in followers, and thus their visibility. We can reflect on forms of precarity linked to this kind of labour – such as being dependent on a mercurial platform – and later generalise this precarity to broader working conditions that involve being visible to others. Prominence is thus enabling, as it can be a means to generate forms of capital (cf. Dupont, 2004) in a professional context by generating financial capital through ad revenue, or exploiting professional networks for cultural or political influence (Arnesson, 2023). Yet prominence also brings heightened vulnerability, through heightened scrutiny and the possibility of intervention from others. We are left asking whether having a high follower count makes someone more susceptible to online attacks such as denunciations and harassment, or more capable of handling such attacks. At this stage, we can speculate that both are valid outcomes.

There are multiple pathways to prominence. The distinction between established and fledgling public figures is characterised by a tension: they all make use of the same platforms in largely similar ways. Yet the quantity of followers they yield brings substantial differences in terms of the typical social impact of these uses. A YouTube celebrity with a million subscribers can easily mobilise even a small fraction of them to harass a target. Depending on the followers' loyalty, they can also weather the professional and financial consequences of being cancelled. A content creator with a few hundred subscribers is in a much more vulnerable position during a public outcry. Followers are a partial liability by bringing greater exposure and scrutiny, but can also be mobilised for strategic and financial ends.

Prominent users like influencers typically seek visibility, and then cope with challenging conditions if they succeed. Brighenti(2007, p. 330) refers to augmented, or super-visibility as a degree of visibility that exceeds what we would collectively – and contextually – consider "fair". Digitally mediated prominence may be generally desirable, insofar as there is also a minimal threshold for fair visibility, below which people are socially excluded. For marginalised groups including racial and sexual minorities, being invisible means being deprived of recognition (ibid., p. 329). What matters is not only visibility, but also agency: empowerment is not just a matter of seeing or being seen, but having control over the conditions in which these occur (ibid., p. 339).

In terms of locating prominent users, we clearly identify them at any mention of influencers. Indeed, influencers embody the aforementioned features and are often associated with online cultural sectors like beauty vloggers (Berryman & Kavka, 2017) and video game streamers (Huang & Morozov, 2022). The category of influencer includes those who not only command a significant following but do so through exclusively their own mediated visibility (cf. Brooks et al., 2021 on celebrities). With influencers, we must recognise a much broader range of aspiring individuals with diminishing reach and influence, who make use of practices and discourses to augment their visibility in a given context. Other figures who feature prominently in contemporary mediated 'public' spheres include politicians, athletes, as well as entertainers such as musicians, comedians and actors. Here too we can work with a sliding scale of prominence, where a minor-league footballer would generate less prominence than a star in a top league but would still embody many of these characteristics. Such a distribution also seems to occur with content creators like young adult novelists, video game live streamers, freelance artists and political commentators.

Beyond these types, we see people who temporarily become internet sensations, such as the undecided American voter whose Reddit history became the subject of scrutiny following his appearance in a 2016 presidential debate.[17] At the margins, we identify nearly anybody who is made visible in their own professional or cultural context. Such prominence may be limited to this local context, but can potentially spill beyond these borders in the case of a public taking offence to their actions. As seen in the previous chapter, there are countless instances of someone angering 'Young Adult Fiction Twitter' or a comparable online community, with the fallout becoming viral beyond that community.[18] In such cases, a cohesive audience-as-community temporarily latches on to a target based on a misdeed, and may continue to follow and scrutinise that person after their public shaming.

Some prominent individuals gather an online following by directing attention to the misdeeds of others. They may frame this content creation as a public service. In the case of *Cittadini Non Distratti* [Citizens Not Distracted], a Venice-based civilian group films themselves shouting at suspected pickpockets. This local concern gained global attention when the voice of one member circulated on TikTok, taking advantage of the platform's ability to reuse audio fragments. While early media coverage focused on the virality of the woman's voice and the nuisance that this group was denouncing, it was soon revealed that she was a municipal councillor of a far-right political party.[19] This revelation led to public backlash against the group and the woman, in the press and on social media. Yet the account remains prominent, with nearly seven hundred thousand followers and twenty-two million likes on TikTok.[20] In some cases, the prominent denunciator's motives may be more ambivalent. The group *Cart Narcs* describes itself as "an independent, non-governmental agency of highly trained agents who have only one desire: that everyone return their shopping cart."[21] Its YouTube channel gathered nearly six hundred thousand subscribers, in part due to the entertaining format put together by its founder, 'Agent Sebastian.' While claiming to "promot[e] considerate behavior" (Reynolds & John, 2021, p. 1), Agent Sebastian also promotes a line of merchandise on his homepage. The spectacular nature of his confrontations led to controversy, which in turn led to further deliberation on his antics across media venues, including the popular American talk show *Dr. Phil*. Not all concerned individuals denouncing others are able – or intend – to amass a viral following. Yet pointing out the misdeeds of others has proven to be a feasible way to engage an audience, as well as critical scrutiny against one's own conduct as a prominent individual.

Individuals denouncing can gain prominence by maintaining accounts where they document, comment on and further stoke online drama, as when Twitter users amass a following by 'screenshotting' and denouncing problematic exchanges online. Yet as we see contemporary media stars also engage in hybrid forms of denunciation when in-person thematic confrontations and punitive acts are recorded by the same group of participants and shared online to magnify the impact of shaming. Prominent examples of such hybrid denunciation are media-savvy groups in Russia that each focus on specific types of crime or moral offence. Here the prominence derived from online visibility is useful for participants for several reasons. The order is not hierarchical: online visibility amplifies punishment as the target is nearly permanently exposed to wide audiences. Visibility is wielded for self-promotion by content creators who wish to appear omnipresent or inspire like-minded formations globally. It can help generate income through monetisation of YouTube channels and sponsorship. It may also grant a degree of immunity in the Russian socio-political sphere, a point we explore in Chapter 5. As one pedophile hunter in Moscow stated "I have so many followers online that I can threaten police officers with exposure. If I report a pedophile and police are inactive, I threaten them to make a post [stating] 'Look this policeman protects pedophiles.'"

We have witnessed an expansion of pathways towards prominence, such as posting viral content, that in turn gets picked up by media networks, that in turn enable others to respond to and directly contact the prominent figure. The prominent individual is necessarily bound to some sort of public collective, like an audience. There is an underlying and persistent framing of fans and audiences as a liability (Wray, 2020), even if other media figures like producers, directors and journalists play a more decisive role in a public figure's career. Relations between "the fan and the star" can be troubling (Brighenti, 2007, p. 334), and the practices that regulate relations between content producers and consumers are further destabilised in contemporary media environments. On YouTube there are many ways a user can provide negative feedback to a prominent figure, including posting comments and response videos. And this is just one of many platforms that audiences can harness against prominent targets.

Influencers and prominent digital media users more generally can be situated in a media landscape that Brighenti characterises as a:

> trade-off between two contradictory visibility forces: the necessity of a renewal in the hall of fame, on the one hand, and the fact that attention of the public is a scarce resource, which focuses only on a bunch of visually easily recognizable media persons, on the other hand. The outcome of this tension is the definition of a field with a nucleus of core, long-standing celebrities, surrounded by a belt of more or less episodic VIPs.
>
> (ibid., p. 334).

Those public figures who do not make up the core of 'A-list' figures struggle with a need for renewal, and competition for attention. In struggling with these demands, prominent users cope with a tension: they are treated as if they have control of their career, for example in tabloids that accuse influencers of causing media outrage.[22] Yet we argue that they wield comparatively little control over audiences, platforms or press. They remain at the mercy of these circumstances, while often framed as responsible for the outcomes that follow.

Prominence is also aligned most closely with what Brighenti calls a media form of visibility: extracted from its original context to a separate one with other cultural and moral expectations. Content may remain legible in its own world and context, yet a "flash-halo mechanism" (ibid., p. 339) extracts someone's behaviour from this context, enabling it to be plugged into other settings. We also recognise aspects of Brighenti's other two forms of being seen in digital media practice. It is social, in that it is enabling, allowing recognition of previously unknown individuals and their grievances. Prominence through digital media visibility is necessary for many kinds of media careers, and indeed these platforms are used for virtually all forms of social interaction. Likewise, it reflects a form of control: digital media visibility is a strategic resource for the regulation and stratification of individuals. It also exists as a kind of strategy to be used against a target when exposing their misdeeds to a broader audience.

Several fundamental reasons compel people to achieve heightened visibility in their social and professional lives, which in turn makes representations of them – and thus, their reputation, their brand, their sponsors and even their friends and family – fluid and spreading to other contexts. This cross-contextual visibility can then be leveraged against them when these representations are scrutinised and denounced in a court of public opinion.

What does cancel culture tell us about prominence?

Cancel culture is a selectively used discourse to frame seemingly negative outcomes for those under public scrutiny. We start from the premise that cancel culture is not contained in the entertainment sector. While those who are more prominent face a heightened risk of being cancelled, the way that we talk about celebrity scandal – and the negative outcomes that follow – can now be extended to a broader public, and we are witnessing that extension in real-time.

The risk of cancellation is part of a generalised struggle with mediated visibility: even if one has a non-cancelled prominence, there are still burdens of having a fandom with which influencers and others cope (Abidin, 2016). Heightened visibility brings heightened scrutiny, and audiences may discover personal details that taint a prominent figure's short-lived fame. Cancellation is thus a surveillant imaginary that has been mainstreamed, shaping how people see themselves and others through digital media, and how they understand audiences as a socio-political force. Rather than reducing relations of visibility to the pairing of "pathological voyeurs with eager narcissists" in a manner that "promotes a joyous affirmation of surveillance" (Kammerer, 2012, p. 106), contemporary stories of cancellation present heightened mediated visibility as both routinised and ambivalent for participants, especially as cases transcend political stripes and professional as well as personal settings. Prominence entails being able to mobilise followers against enemies and other targets, but also being targeted by such mobilisations, including by one's own following.

What happens to prominent figures in cancellation is not fundamentally different from the social justice and abuse delivered to targets in Chapter 2. The way people react to cancel culture suggests a firming up of longstanding practices to 'manage' prominent individuals. A recent antecedent are the strategies young users adopted in response to lateral surveillance on social media platforms (Duffy & Chan, 2019). Cancel culture is made meaningful with high-profile cases, in turn providing a set of expectations and vocabulary for minor entertainers slightly removed from celebrity status, as well as those with little connection to the world of celebrity.

Below we provide an overview of cancel culture in relation to visible (counter-)denunciation. It must be said that cancel culture has many other societal implications, including political ideology (Norris, 2023), media censorship (Hidy, 2021), marketing (Saldanha et al., 2023) and property rights (Bagus et al., 2023). Cancel culture discourses are emblematic of pressing social issues, while at the same time can also be dismissed as trend-chasing editorials. Cancel culture matters for many reasons, including tracking relations between media visibility and reputation. Cancel culture can be more concretely defined as a mediated denunciation in which a prominent public figure such as an entertainer is denounced for recent or previous misdeeds. This is followed by a collective decision to rescind public support, with direct financial impacts when no longer consuming content that they produce. While less explicitly and criminally harmful than other forms of retaliation like doxing and death threats, the target's career and public standing is thus hobbled by a lessened reputation and diminished engagement. This specific use of the term cancelled takes its origins in African-American culture, including the 1991 film *New Jack City* and later in the reality television programme *Love and Hip-Hop* as well as by Black Twitter accounts (Ng, 2022). Cancellation discourse garnered a broad audience who then appropriated this term in other settings. It became further popularised in the context of progressive and identity-based movements, especially as these play out in mainstream news and entertainment media.

Cancel culture mobilises a wide and diverse network of supporters. Even if the denouncer seeks a proportionate response (for example in the quantity and severity of replies), their followers and a broader public can further amplify denunciations beyond proportionality. Mediated denunciation also implicates the social network of targets, including their associates, collaborators, sponsors, employers, co-workers and relatives. Its proponents claim to seek to separate a target from their support networks, especially from those who can provide material support, like employers. On first pass, this resembles an attempt for consumers to exert agency, not only in terms of producing content, or having dissenting readings of media texts, but in seeking to remove targeted media actors, and the content associated with them. Early prominent cases emerged in Hollywood and on Instagram, denouncing sexual abuse. This is especially evident in the wake of #MeToo, as a collective call to stop financially supporting sexual predators in the entertainment industry. Denunciation also occurred during #BLM protests, where footage of African-Americans murdered by police not only led to calls to defund police forces, but also greater scrutiny of racist content by entertainers, including YouTube celebrities and other social media influencers, as well as individuals with a limited public presence.

Fundamentally, cancellation as a social phenomenon is a collective withdrawal of support, be it attention, engagement, goodwill or money. This has an obvious application to celebrity culture, and shares features with a more general corporate boycotting of brands and companies (cf. Jacquet, 2015). In practice, it is partly aligned with other consumer-based political tactics: individual reputations may be consumed, as both a collective strategy to effect social change, and as a media strategy to capture attention and engagement on a given platform. Yet the scope of potential targets extends indefinitely to other professional sectors, and to private civilians who are either public-facing for their careers or are launched into the public eye through the acts of other observers.

There are numerous examples of prominent entertainers who have been the target of cancellation, including Harvey Weinstein and Kevin Spacey following revelations of sexual misconduct. In some cases, cancellation was an opportunity to revisit long-standing public denunciations, as with Woody Allen and R. Kelly. These celebrities faced the closest approximation of a contemporary status degradation, where they are ostensibly revealed to be as "he was all along" (Garfinkel, 1956, p. 422). In other words, these disgraced entertainers may attempt to rehabilitate their reputation, but these efforts are in response to their newly lowered status, as opposed to an attempt to circumvent this downgrade. Even for figures that have always been mired in controversy, contemporary cancellation marks a categorical shift in their public status, and thus their ability to operate in their professional community. Roseanne Barr, who has faced public backlash for decades (Dresner, 1993), published a racist tweet in 2018 that led to denunciation by journalists and other media figures. Hers is a more explicit instance of cancellation, as her eponymous television show was also cancelled, with the supporting cast turning to a spin-off called *The Connors*. An article from *The Guardian* entitled "Roseanne cancelled" denotes both the show and the star as impacted by cancel culture.[23]

As nationalist shaming rises in China, many prominent content creators embrace the logic of the engagement economy by producing content that stirs up nationalism among Chinese audiences. This trend has not gone unnoticed by the wider public. As Chinese citizens' media literacy increases, there are mounting criticisms of content creators' opportunism. For example, six Sina Weibo accounts that initiated public denunciation against "traitors" have been jokingly dubbed "The Okamoto [a Japanese condom brand] Six" as they all had a sponsorship deal with the Japanese brand in their earlier posts, while doxing and shaming Chinese girls photographed wearing kimonos while abroad.[24] State media like CCTV also commented on the proliferation of content creators reporting on "unpatriotic behaviour" with an explicitly harsh tone in titles such as: "patriotism should not be a business; reporting should be fact-based."[25]

While we focus on the role of the state in Chapter 5, in countries like China and Russia their interventions may be unavoidable in prominent cases of cancellation. Cancel culture in Russia brought heightened levels of polarisation after the full-scale invasion of Ukraine in 2022. Artists and public figures became instruments of state propaganda to normalise the status quo and inspire 'patriotic' sentiments. Some artists immediately denounced the war and left Russia. Others attempted a cautious 'business as usual' approach by avoiding any public statements about the invasion. A third category of passionate supporters of the regime and its war (referred to as a "special military operation" in Russia) were the so-called 'Z-artists.' As international conflict grew, some countries opted to cancel concerts for the Z-artists,[26] while others cancelled those critical of the regime.[27] Within Russia, the state launched a public reputational execution of artists who 'cautiously' avoided vocal support. In December 2023, the state invoked notions of morality to accuse prominent figures of living in a parallel reality for attending the so-called "almost naked party" while soldiers were dying for the motherland.[28] A deluge of public apologies followed. Nevertheless, many of the artists were cut from New Year's entertainment shows, and their ability to generate income inside Russia fell in jeopardy. To regain public and state trust, some travelled to the occupied territories in Ukraine and gave concerts there.

Following cancellation, prominent figures may experience continued sanctions on media platforms. Yet the supposed exclusion from the media sector is not always evident, as a celebrity can simply assert that they were cancelled[29] while remaining in the public eye. Prominent individuals can turn to public relations tools and practices to assert control over their personal public narrative. In doing so they may retain part of their former audience, and also gain new followers who are ideologically opposed to whatever social cause led to their cancellation.[30] Those who have been cancelled or downgraded may enter a hostile and perpetually uphill struggle with regard to their mediated visibility and reputation, as any attempt to regain prominence will be met with a continued denunciation of the past offences that led to their cancellation. Yet with the recent mainstreaming of claims of cancellation, prominent figures may simply claim to experience this struggle, especially if they wish to tap into a politically polarised fanbase.

Cancel culture and prominent criticisms

Cancel culture can be understood as a public denunciation of someone. In turn, those accused of participating in cancel culture are openly criticised, most prominently in conservative media.[31] Cancel culture's detractors refer to an ever-changing moral threshold of offence taking, as well as a lack of proportionality in punishments against transgressors. This public discourse marks a moment when controversial media practices are made meaningful, notably when prominent forms of denunciation are themselves prominently denounced. These complaints are primarily based on perceived ideological drivers behind these denunciations, and in turn support an ideologically selective account of what counts as legitimate grievance. The practices implicated by these debates are much broader than typically framed, as one can find similar repertoires mobilised by those who prominently claim to oppose cancel culture. There are also criticisms of cancel culture as a form of "trial-by-mob" justice,[32] where notions of proportionality and rehabilitation are compromised due to a collective fervour against the offending act. This commentary risks overlooking the diversity of cancellation cases, and thus a diversity of outcomes ranging from socially acceptable to disproportionate. Members of the so-called 'woke mob' seek career-ending sanction and jail time for longstanding sexual predators in positions of power like Harvey Weinstein. Yet they may not consider the same punishment appropriate for a minor figure facing much less damning allegations.

Conservative media outlets have denounced cancel culture, and this has gained popular prominence in the context of broader so-called 'culture wars.' These critiques of cancel culture gain prominence with an open letter in *Harper's Magazine*[33] that does not denounce cancel culture explicitly, but is widely recognised as a pushback to this phenomenon.[34] It is worth noting that signatories of the open letter include public figures who engage in similar practices of denouncing opponents.[35] The *Harper's* letter can be interpreted as journalists and prominent public figures tending to their reputational wounds in public.[36] This in turn amplifies cancel culture as a talking point, as opposed to focusing on underlying social and political accelerants of online harms. This open letter effectively serves as a call for free speech by media actors who disproportionately shape public discourse. It arguably reflects an attempt to assert control over the mediated expression of public opinion, under the guise of defending a liberal "free exchange of information and ideas."[37] In the next chapter, we further consider the role of the press in upholding online shitstorms as the most viable format of the court of public opinion.

Many editorials and news pieces bring scrutiny and denunciation under scrutiny, including denunciatory voices of others. This is also evident in titles such as "YouTubers are calling out the platform's 'cancel culture.'"[38] This article goes on to distinguish two types of YouTube channels that exploit public denunciations: those that are strictly "opinions of the drama and their personal feeling towards the influencer they are speaking about" and "receipt based" ones that "are usually anonymous and lay down the various sagas in a factual, step-by-step slideshow of screenshots and captions." Within this sub-community, we already see a tiering of those who merely express their grievances, and those who make use of screenshots and other data sourced from the target's account, among other locations. As seen in Chapter 1, the implication in this quote is that receipt-based denunciations are legitimated as more methodical, more fact-based and therefore more trustworthy.

These criticisms largely present cancel culture as a bottom-up phenomenon, as if only internet users are responsible. This framing overlooks media actors who exert greater influence and resources, including those who manage platforms, those who choose to fire targets, those that fund or publicise content creators and those who configure algorithms that promote this content. Press coverage may present Twitter users as a singular form of social pressure to ruin people's lives, instead of a temporary assembly of actors with vastly diverse ideological beliefs and goals. Online shitstorms are composed of individuals who may be economically and politically marginalised. They are framed as causing civil unrest and instability when they call for an editor to be fired, and this demand is actually met. Journalists and other public figures may denounce those engaging in cancel culture. In doing so they may call for proponents to face social sanction that highly resembles cancellation. Here retaliation against cancel culture amounts to more status degradation, and further public engagement that fuels press and platforms' economic engine, a point that is also explored in the next chapter.

Bottom-up, lateral and top-down denunciations share a public attempt to punish a target by harming their livelihood by way of their reputation and employment. And while conservative critics frame cancellation as a left-leaning phenomenon, this is a broader feature of interactions through digital media, especially in the context of political contestation, or simply as a source of entertainment. The court of public opinion is fundamentally about sourcing information about people, whereas the actual deliberation of their social worth and outcome seems to be obviated as a judicial step. Selected forms of denunciation are flagged as disruptive and troubling practices. Cancel culture denotes an ever-changing set of conditions in which the public interact with and take steps to either support or condemn celebrities and other public figures. These practices assert that public figures are only in positions of power and privilege because of the public who serve as a regular audience and occasionally provide financial backing. One way this is articulated is through claims that a public audience supports the targeted individual, and therefore has the right to withdraw that support.

In a separate turn, criticisms of cancel culture are also criticised, in part because they invoke a discriminatory and contradictory account of social sanction, while overlooking other longstanding equivalents.[39] While these editorials are published, a steady stream of reports feature prominent individuals denounced for actionable conduct, including inappropriate speech. These incidents fuel more think pieces and keep the topic of online shaming in the public eye. Across cultures, we witness a renegotiation of appropriate digital media conduct, namely addressing the conditions in which it is permitted to publicly denounce someone. If we accept the premise that cancel culture is a kind of moral panic about offensive content and behaviour, then it stands to reason that the denunciation of cancel culture is the most recent iteration of "moral panic about moral panics" (Cree et al., 2016, p. 355), as stated in Chapter 1.

Callout culture as parallel practice

Before cancel culture graced newspaper headlines, callout culture was a prominent topic among activist communities online. Calling out refers to the practice of denouncing someone's objectionable behaviour as a public exposition. In their mainstreaming, these terms tend to overlap with each other as mediated denunciations. Also emerging from Black counterpublic accountability practices (Clark, 2020), callouts are recently entangled in the management and policing of activist communities, especially if that community is striving for progressive goals. This follows a tendency for ideological vanguards and potentially vulnerable communities more generally to self-police as a matter of self-preservation (cf. Madsen, 2004).

Callouts are widely understood as being performative.[40] Not only do denunciations typically end up being public, they are often mediated, either directly, or are later recounted online. These criticisms claim that callouts reflect disparities in the time and other privileges necessary to avoid doing anything that would lead to a callout, especially access to activist and academic spaces. While racism and sexual abuse are indefensible, being late to adopt more inclusive language – including terms that may be previously unknown in certain communities – is both understandable and repairable. As a rejoinder to being called out, many writers and activists proposed "calling in" as an alternative.[41] This distinction echoes Braithwaite's (1989) dichotomy of stigmatisation versus reintegrative forms of shaming, with the latter enabling an offender to eventually participate in community life. The possibility of reintegration assumes a safe environment for accusations like sexual abuse to be addressed, and that existing power dynamics would not simply favour an abuser in power. It also assumes that there is a cohesive community that can watch over or attend to the target. This may be the case with an activist group that has a clearly expressed possibility for reintegration (Abraham, 2013). It may also be possible within professional contexts (Arroyo-Ramirez et al., 2018). Yet more recently the mainstreaming of callouts and cancellation claims pushes these accusations and deliberations into a much broader public sphere. The possibility of deliberation and re-integration of a target seems unsustainable in such environments. With this mainstreaming, it remains as feasible as ever for people to bring material harm to a target, such as loss of employment or revenue. But the steps that would conclude a denunciation, whether rehabilitative or exclusionary, are less tangible.

Whereas callout culture appears to be rooted in activist circles, cancel culture is prominently aligned with entertainment and fandoms. Between callout and cancel culture, we can interpret that cancellation is meant to denounce on behalf of a wider population. Callout culture suggests the risk of being banished from one's community, while early formulations of cancellation were meant to target prominent Hollywood celebrities, presumably from the perspective of a global audience. With callout culture there is the assumption that the denouncer and target may belong to the same social circle. This is not assumed in cancel culture. In the case of entertainers, denunciation and its material impact are often framed as if the collective that is rejecting the target had previously supported them by consuming their content. Yet it may be the case that they had no prior engagement with the figure being denounced.

Both cancel and callout culture respond to the use of potentially hateful and hurtful language, as both have a progressive ideological framing. Both deal with the question of how to identify a person who is deemed to be objectionable, and how to handle that person with regards to their social status. This includes what a community and a targeted individual respectively owe one another. Here we find a distinction between callout and cancel culture, with callout culture offering more potential for rehabilitation. The fact that both occur through digital media, and that conversations about them are also taking place through these platforms facilitates a confluence between social justice and progressive audiences, but also well beyond these audiences. This is why cancel culture is denounced by *Fox News* and other partisan media, but also co-opted by many right-leaning venues. Even callouts that are localised to specific communities and digital spaces risk becoming visible on a grand scale when picked up by other networks and venues, for instance when a member of a niche hobby community writes about a recent scandal in a more mainstream media venue.

Much like cancel culture, callouts are subject to mis- or re-interpretation. A *Forbes* article on "callout culture" frames it primarily in terms of customer complaints.[42] This is not surprising, as new terms are introduced to diverse contexts, at which point their meaning may become diluted. Despite distinct origins, there is an overlap between cancel and callout culture, as seen when celebrities are at once described as called out[43] and cancelled.[44] With time, both callout culture and cancel culture practices become embedded in extremely online cultures that in turn facilitate uncharitable interpretations of both strangers and peers as a default social lens.

Conclusion

The language of cancel culture can be extended to anyone who may live partly or substantially in the public eye. This includes individuals who are dependent on public support, such as those using crowdfunding platforms like GoFundme to fund healthcare costs, or Patreon to seek freelance work (Hunter, 2016). Less prominent people are also 'cancelled' when facing sanctions in their professional and personal lives. What we mean by public – being both a beneficiary of being visible, and thus being considered fair game for scrutiny and denunciation – is also changing. One concern is that it is not just people who want to be in a position of prominent visibility: many are compelled to do so because of workplace demands and economic hardship. Visibility becomes "relentless" (Ganesh, 2016). Facing these anxieties, cancel culture has become a prevailing surveillant imaginary. People may cope with a mounting sense of vulnerability through digital media in part by learning about how mediated visibility harms prominent figures through cancellations. Shaming and denunciation are fundamental tools of influence and coercion in all social contexts. The general process of cancellation is not new. Yet we can observe a ratcheting up of practices, or a consolidation of disparate forms of denunciation under a more unified banner. This occurs alongside a dispersal of the term 'cancel' to re-imagine justice and retribution against wrongdoings among people, especially those who may be under the public eye. Cancellation means withdrawing support, and its application now extends to less prominent people who garner public support on a lesser scale. Looking at press coverage and public discourse, cancel culture is typically situated in an entertainment context, and readers should remain attentive to how it is also implicitly and explicitly utilised to make sense of other settings.

Media figures use the term cancel culture in a way that exceeds reasonable definitions of the practice. This dispersal speaks to confluence between celebrity culture and interpersonal communication (cf. Hearn, 2008), such that we witness a "broadening of what counts as a public figure" (Márquez-Reiter & Haugh, 2019, p. 35). Many public figures are low-level or aspiring celebrities. And more generally other interpersonal interactions are reframed in the light of celebrity exposure. Yet it is likely that even less pronounced cases of cancellation endure as a stain on people's reputation and public standing. Denunciations may be obscured when more recent content about other people push a post further down a social platform's news feed. In a typical Reddit community, if a post is a few days old, it is already deep in the archives. Yet for a motivated and minimally skilled internet user, it can be dug up at any point in a tactical attempt to harm someone.

Prominent users and ordinary individuals share an ambivalence with mediated visibility as both a pathway to capital and a pervasive social vulnerability. This risk is especially vexing for prominent individuals to manage, as it involves other people knowingly or unknowingly bringing harm to the target before the camera. In establishing a prominent social media profile by "cultivating social relationships as 'followers,' 'friends,' and 'connections'" (Duffy & Chan, 2019, p. 134), other people subscribe to and circulate a prominent figure's content. Media users in front of a camera may accumulate detractors by making controversial content visible and accessible. In addition to strangers becoming anti-fans (Gray, 2003), fans may take exception to some content themselves and join anti-fandoms. Followers may also misbehave, reflecting badly on the public figure.[45] Visibility is a trap (Foucault, 1977), but it is also a paycheque. One takeaway is that it is preferable to receive a paycheque off someone else's visibility. In the next chapter, we focus on media platforms that host the court of public opinion.

Notes

1 https://www.narcity.com/fr/le-compte-instagram-cancelinfluenceurs-dnonce-les-influenceurs-et-explose-en-popularit
2 https://www.instagram.com/p/CJq5_IAH1qh/
3 https://www.cliqueduplateau.com/2021/01/07/linfluenceuse-qui-regarde-la-covid-19-dans-lsud/
4 https://www.newstatesman.com/science-tech/2020/07/cancel-culture-does-not-exist
5 https://nypost.com/2022/04/30/professors-on-how-they-were-canceled-why-they-fought-back/
6 https://www.linkedin.com/pulse/cancel-culture-cant-my-business-theresa-robertson
7 https://www.npr.org/2021/07/02/1012696671/co-opted-and-weaponized-cancel-culture-is-just-todays-politically-correct
8 This is a term that is often used in English-speaking and Dutch contexts for people who spend too much time online, and shape their cultural and political beliefs from things like Twitter arguments, which they may deem as important as flagship news sources. See for example: https://www.indymedia.nl/node/48727.
9 https://www.bbc.com/worklife/article/20210226-the-darkly-soothing-compulsion-of-doomscrolling
10 https://static.nytimes.com/email-content/INT_4981.html
11 https://xkcd.com/386/
12 https://mashable.com/article/log-off-touch-grass
13 https://www.bbc.com/news/world-us-canada-65553608
14 https://www.theguardian.com/lifeandstyle/2016/jan/21/gomi-blog-internet-comments-women
15 This visibility led to controversy in the case of Twitter when, under Elon Musk's rule, view counts per tweet also became visible: https://www.socialmediatoday.com/news/Twitter-Launches-Updated-Tweet-View-Count-Display/640549/. Among other outcomes, this brought new practices of measuring and mocking tweets that had a low view-to-engagement ratio.
16 https://time.com/6258607/you-time-person-of-the-year-2006/
17 https://www.washingtonpost.com/news/the-intersect/wp/2016/10/14/ken-bone-was-a-hero-now-ken-bone-is-bad-it-was-his-destiny-as-a-human-meme/. See also discourse about 'Milkshake Duck': https://www.vox.com/culture/22350188/what-is-a-milkshake-duck-definition-explained-jensen-karp-cinnamon-toast-shrimp
18 https://www.newyorker.com/books/under-review/in-ya-where-is-the-line-between-criticism-and-cancel-culture
19 https://www.nytimes.com/2023/07/25/style/attenzione-pickpocket.html
20 While the account in question claims to be the 'official' one, it should be noted that there are at least twenty-two accounts bearing the group's name on TikTok, with four others making a similar claim. The second most popular account has twenty-nine thousand followers, while the remaining ones range from zero to fifty followers.
21 http://cartnarcs.com/about.html
22 https://www.dailymail.co.uk/news/article-12274727/Influencer-pretends-pick-rubbish-beach-radio-host-Deanne-Carbonne-denies-her.html
23 https://www.theguardian.com/culture/2018/may/29/roseanne-barr-tweet-valerie-jarrett-ape
24 https://chinadigitaltimes.net/chinese/685857.html
25 https://weibo.com/ttarticle/p/show?id=2309404995105898496153

26 https://central.asia-news.com/en_GB/articles/cnmi_ca/features/2023/06/30/feature-01
27 https://www.themoscowtimes.com/2023/06/20/moscow-warns-kyiv-against-targeting-crimea-with-western-arms-a81570
28 https://www.plovism.com/post/oops-when-the-regime-comes-after-your-ass
29 https://newrepublic.com/article/158535/self-cancellation-bari-weiss
30 https://www.thedailybeast.com/mel-gibson-is-living-proof-that-cancel-culture-is-mostly-bullshit
31 https://www.washingtonpost.com/politics/2020/01/14/fox-news-talks-about-cancel-culture-political-correctness-lot-more-than-its-competitors/
32 https://nypost.com/2020/02/02/ridiculous-attacks-on-american-dirt-are-fresh-reason-to-nix-cancel-culture/
33 https://harpers.org/a-letter-on-justice-and-open-debate/
34 https://www.latimes.com/entertainment-arts/story/2020-07-09/cancel-culture-harpers-letter
35 https://www.thenation.com/article/archive/why-is-the-op-ed-page-of-the-new-york-times-obsessed-with-college-kids/
36 https://quillette.com/2020/07/09/it-wasnt-my-cancelation-that-bothered-me-it-was-the-cowardice-of-those-who-let-it-happen/
37 https://harpers.org/a-letter-on-justice-and-open-debate/
38 https://www.insider.com/cancel-culture-what-it-means-creators-on-youtube-2019-9
39 https://www.theroot.com/the-misplaced-hysteria-about-a-cancel-culture-that-do-1829563238
40 https://www.nytimes.com/2019/10/31/us/politics/obama-woke-cancel-culture.html
41 https://briarpatchmagazine.com/articles/view/a-note-on-call-out-culture
42 https://www.forbes.com/sites/petersuciu/2020/01/08/social-medias-callout-culture-continues-to-improve-customer-service/#5b28651b6d99
43 https://www.buzzfeednews.com/article/michaelblackmon/shane-gillis-racist-comments-snl
44 https://www.thedailybeast.com/shane-gillis-is-netflixs-1-comedian-4-years-after-snl-firing
45 https://www.vox.com/policy-and-politics/2020/3/9/21168312/bernie-bros-bernie-sanders-chapo-trap-house-dirtbag-left. In the case of the 'Bernie Bros' we need to acknowledge that this label is arguably amplified as a weapon against a progressive political candidate, all while claims made against his more problematic supporters online may also be valid.

References

Abidin, C. (2016). Visibility labour: Engaging with Influencers' fashion brands and #OOTD advertorial campaigns on Instagram. *Media International Australia, 161*(1), 86–100. https://doi.org/10.1177/1329878x16665177

Abidin, C. (2021). Mapping internet celebrity on TikTok: Exploring attention economies and visibility labours. *Cultural Science Journal, 12*(1), 77–103. https://doi.org/10.5334/csci.140

Abraham, B. (2013). Fedora shaming as discursive activism. *Digital Culture & Education, 5*(2), 86–97. http://hdl.handle.net/10453/41907

Arnesson, J. (2023). Influencers as ideological intermediaries: Promotional politics and authenticity labour in influencer collaborations. *Media, Culture & Society, 45*(3), 528–44. https://doi.org/10.1177/01634437221117505

Arroyo-Ramirez, E., Chou, R. L., Freedman, J., Fujita, S., & Orozco, C. M. (2018). The reach of a long-arm stapler: Calling in microaggressions in the LIS field through zine work. *Library Trends*, *67*(1), 107–130. https://doi.org/10.1353/lib.2018.0028

Bagus, P., Daumann, F., & Follert, F. (2023). Microaggressions, cancel culture, safe spaces, and academic freedom: A private property rights argumentation. *Business Ethics, the Environment & Responsibility*. https://doi.org/10.1111/beer.12626

Berryman, R., & Kavka, M. (2017). 'I guess a lot of people see me as a big sister or a friend': The role of intimacy in the celebrification of beauty vloggers. *Journal of Gender Studies*, *26*(3), 307–320. https://doi.org/10.1080/09589236.2017.1288611

Braithwaite, J. (1989). *Crime, shame and reintegration*. Cambridge University Press. https://doi.org/10.1017/cbo9780511804618

Brighenti, A. (2007). Visibility: A category for the social sciences. *Current Sociology*, *55(*3), 323–342. https://doi.org/10.1177/0011392107076079

Clark, M. D. (2020). DRAG THEM: A brief etymology of so-called "cancel culture". *Communication and the Public*, *5*(3–4), 88–92. https://doi.org/10.1177/2057047320961562

Cree, V. E., Clapton, G., & Smith, M. (2016). Standing up to complexity: Researching moral panics in social work. *European Journal of Social Work*, *19*(3–4), 354–367. https://doi.org/10.4324/9781315206929-5

Daviess, B. (2019) 'Making memes and shitposting': The powerful political discourse of alt-right meme culture. https://ssrn.com/abstract=4118990

Dresner, Z. Z. (1993). Roseanne barr: Goddess or she-devil. *Journal of American Culture*, *16*(2), 37–44. https://doi.org/10.1111/j.1542-734x.1993.00037.x

Duffy, B. E., & Chan, N. K. (2019). "You never really know who's looking": Imagined surveillance across social media platforms. *New Media & Society*, *21*(1), 119–138. https://doi.org/10.1177/1461444818791318

Dupont, B. (2004). Security in the age of networks. *Policing and Society*, *14*(1), 76–91. https://doi.org/10.1080/1043946042000181575

Foucault, M. (1977). *Discipline and punish: The birth of the prison*. Vintage Books.

Garfinkel, H. (1956). Conditions of successful degradation ceremonies.*American Journal of Sociology*, *61*(5), 420–424. https://doi.org/10.1086/221800

Ganesh, S. (2016). Managing surveillance: Surveillant individualism in an era of relentless visibility. *International Journal of Communication, 10*, 164–177. https://ijoc.org/index.php/ijoc/article/view/4544

Gray, J. (2003). New audiences, new textualities: Anti-fans and non-fans. *International Journal of Cultural Studies*, *6*(1), 64–81. https://doi.org/10.1177/1367877903006001004

Hearn, A. (2008). 'Meat, mask, burden': Probing the contours of the branded 'self'. *Journal of Consumer Culture*, *8*(2), 197–217. https://doi.org/10.1177/1469540508090086

Heemstra, J. M. (2020). A scientist's guide to social media. *ACS Central Science*, *6*(1), 1–5. https://doi.org/10.1021/acscentsci.9b01273

Hidy, K. M. (2021). The speech gods: Freedom of speech, censorship, and cancel culture in the age of social media. *Washburn Law Journal*, *61*, 99–161. https://heinonline.org/HOL/P?h=hein.journals/wasbur61&i=107

Huang, Y., & Morozov, I. (2022). Video advertising by twitch influencers. https://ssrn.com/abstract=4065064.

Hunter, A. (2016). "It's like having a second full-time job": Crowdfunding, journalism and labour. *Journalism Practice*, *10*(2), 217–232. https://doi.org/10.1080/17512786.2015.1123107

Jacquet, J. (2015). *Is shame necessary?: New uses for an old tool.* Penguin.

Kammerer, D. (2012). Surveillance in literature, film and television. In K. Ball, K. Haggerty, & D. Lyon (Eds.), *Routledge handbook of surveillance studies* (pp. 99–106). Routledge. https://doi.org/10.4324/9780203814949.ch1_3_c

Madsen, M. L. (2004). Living for home: Policing immorality among undocumented migrants in Johannesburg. *African Studies*, *63*(2), 173–192. https://doi.org/10.1080/00020180412331318742

Márquez-Reiter, R., & Haugh, M. (2019). Denunciation, blame and the moral turn in public life. *Discourse, Context & Media*, *28*, 35–43. https://doi.org/10.1016/j.dcm.2018.09.001

Marwick, A. E. (2013). *Status update: Celebrity, publicity, and branding in the social media age*. Yale University Press. https://doi.org/10.12987/9780300199154

McKelvey, F., & Hunt, R. (2019). Discoverability: Toward a definition of content discovery through platforms. *Social Media + Society*, *5*(1). https://doi.org/10.1177/2056305118819188

Nakamura, L. (2015). The unwanted labour of social media: Women of colour call out culture as venture community management. *New Formations*, *86*(86), 106–112. https://doi-org.eur.idm.oclc.org/10.3898/NEWF.86.06.2015

Norris, P. (2023). Cancel culture: Myth or reality?. *Political Studies*, *71*(1), 145–174. https://doi.org/10.1177/00323217211037023

Ng, E. (2022). *Cancel culture: A critical analysis*. Palgrave Macmillan. https://doi.org/10.1007/978-3-030-97374-2

Paasonen, S., Light, B., & Jarrett, K. (2019). The dick pic: Harassment, curation, and desire. *Social Media + Society*, *5*(2). https://doi.org/10.1177/2056305119826126

Phillips, W. (2015). *This is why we can't have nice things: Mapping the relationship between online trolling and mainstream culture*. MIT Press. https://doi.org/10.7551/mitpress/10288.001.0001

Reynolds, C. J., & John, N. (2021). Cart Narcs and the engineering of social shaming as entertainment. *AoIR Selected Papers of Internet Research.* https://doi.org/10.5210/spir.v2021i0.12232

Rønn, K. V., Hartmann, M. R. K., Diderichsen, A., Ralph, L., & Trottier, D. (2024). The crafting of an online police métier. *The case of Norwegian Online Police Patrols.* Manuscript under review.

Saldanha, N., Mulye, R., & Rahman, K. (2023). Cancel culture and the consumer: A strategic marketing perspective. *Journal of Strategic Marketing*, *31*(5), 1071–1086. https://doi.org/10.1080/0965254x.2022.2040577

Scaratti, G., & Cortini, M. (2013). Using social network as organizational storytelling: A narrative analysis of dooced employees' blogs. In P. Spagnoletti (Ed.), *Organizational change and information systems: Working and living together in new ways* (pp. 225–231). Springer. https://doi.org/10.1007/978-3-642-37228-5_22

Sobolewska, M., & Ford, R. (2020). Brexit and Britain's culture wars. *Political Insight*, *11*(1), 4–7. https://doi.org/10.1177/2041905820911738

Wray, R. (2020). # NotMyFandom: The gendered nature of a misogynistic backlash in science fiction fandom. *Psychology of Women and Equalities Review*, *3*(1&2), 78–81. https://doi.org/10.53841/bpspowe.2020.3.1–2.78

4 Who runs the media?

The role of platforms and the press

On being the 'main character' on the internet

> [T]witter is 90% someone imagining a guy, tricking themselves into believing that guy exists and then getting mad about it[1]
>
> If this is you: F**k you

On platforms like Reddit, digital media users are likely to encounter broad denunciations like the one quoted above. It accompanied a photo taken at a grocery store, featuring multiple people with shopping carts overflowing with economy-sized packages of toilet paper. This post was not denouncing or pursuing a single person, but instead targeted a broader category of problematic behaviour, namely the hoarding of household goods. Unlike focusing on a single person, addressing a category scales up to denouncing a broader social problem. The accusers can evade scrutiny of their denunciation when referring to a 'type of person' instead of a single event from which one may expect evidence and context. It may not be the case that people hoarding toilet paper correspond to the imagined 'type of person,' yet they are made meaningful in public discourse in a way that crowdsources authorship of incidents to anybody willing to post or comment on the matter, while also giving platforms and their clients control over how that content is arranged, accessed and retained. These posts do not resemble a public trial, compared to the targeted denunciations covered earlier in this book. A judgment is still being made, but even the previously flimsy pretence of deliberation is dropped. Rather, this example suggests a step further towards entertainment-based media practice. Platforms like Reddit and Twitter enable data sharing about people in ways that other users will find agreeable or disagreeable, though never neutral, as indifference and disinterest do not benefit platforms in an engagement economy.

Denunciatory posts are user-led, based on user-generated content and are curated, solicited and managed by media entities, in this case, a private company from California. Reddit's economic viability depends on sustained user activity, including authoring posts and comments. This input in turn generates advertising revenue and other forms of monetisation. Engagement matters, and one way to engage people is through appeals to a sense of injustice

DOI: 10.4324/9781003453017-4

or revulsion, especially if linking this content to additional appeals such as humour, disgust or lust (Hesmondhalgh, 2010). Platforms like Facebook, Twitter and Reddit (but also those in other sectors like Uber and Airbnb) operate by enabling and convincing users to engage and provide something of value to other users. This includes prominent content creators like authors, artists, influencers, models and vloggers, as well as unremarkable people posting to their social networks. And unremarkable content may also end up provoking viral outrage and finding a similar reach as those from more prominent users.

Nobody wants to deal with the fallout of being the "main character" on Twitter,[2] or any other media platform. Consider the person who briefly became the most hated man in Australia when triggering a six-day statewide lockdown (Trottier et al., 2021). Tabloid articles reporting on this case perform a dual function of both denouncing an individual based on rhetoric, whilst reporting on a broader social denunciation of that same person via screenshots of vitriolic comments. Here the press are co-creating a denunciatory event, in conjunction with digital platforms. This includes repurposing online interactions as tabloid content, either capturing source material from Twitter or sharing screenshots already in circulation. Screenshots are a communicative and epistemological foot in the door: a digital artefact that users may privilege as consequential. These 'receipts' serve to remediate vitriolic comments, and often help cultivate further comments on their own sites as well as platforms like Facebook where article links may be posted in countless groups. The press can also integrate tweets directly into articles, ensuring recent exchanges and pile-ons are one click away for an enraged and therefore engaged readership.

The court of public opinion as online shitstorms

Media users play a pivotal role in the court of public opinion when generating content about each other. Yet when clicking on 'send' and 'share' they of course depend on the platform – and its owners and operators – to carry out these functions. Although platform valuation is partially based on user presence and input, they are not the primary actors who keep the infrastructure functioning in a technical or procedural sense. As media platforms, Facebook, Reddit and Twitter manage courts of public opinion in ways that used to be dominated by public and private press and broadcasters. This chapter extends from research on tabloid accounts of online justice-seeking (Trottier, 2020) to consider how the press also sustain audience engagement by reporting on online denunciation. They depend on social media, both as a source of content for reports and editorials, and to promote these articles to readers. In addition to their ownership of legacy media venues, they often reach an audience through practices that are comparable to prominent users on social media.

Media platforms, the press and other content farms (Bakker, 2012) exploit people's public standing as a business model. While focusing mainly on digital media platforms, when talking about the media landscape we also acknowledge newspapers and other legacy media as key actors.

After focusing on conventional and prominent users in the last two chapters, we can further address the broader media landscape in which the court of public opinion is usually enacted. We recognise that the court of public opinion largely and historically relies on media platforms and institutions that facilitate them (Lawrence & Bennett, 2001; Foos & Bischof, 2022). It is possible to imagine public opinion manifest without media, such as when a group of activists discusses a predatory colleague in a face-to-face meeting. Yet today even hyper-local and close-knit communities depend on digital platforms like WhatsApp to watch and deliberate over each other. Digital platforms bind family, friends, peers and colleagues on a micro scale, and larger swaths of the public on a broader scale. These platforms exist to collect as much personal data as possible, which is in turn to be exploited in any marketable capacity. As a result, they engage users through the personal data of others. Some of these platforms are considered walled gardens (Clarke, 2014) that prevent data from being exported or shared on other platforms. If Meta's owners had their way, all facets of social life would remain within the boundaries of Facebook, Instagram and WhatsApp. Yet it remains possible for users to scale these walls, for example by using screenshots to spread content to other sites and other networks. And while Western platforms may have limited to no official presence in countries like Russia and China, user-led denunciation and shaming are instead performed through local services. In Russia, many of the so-called global giants are deemed extremist and have domestic alternatives. VKontakte is an alternative to Facebook, Rutube to YouTube, Yandex to Google, etc. Interestingly, the seemingly 'Russian platform' Telegram has only recently become welcome within its national borders after enduring years of state sanction. In China, services like Sina Weibo and WeChat are more than alternatives to Silicon Valley platforms, given how further embedded they are in everyday social and economic contexts. Various competing sites can therefore make up a wider ecosystem for circulating content that condemns others. These platforms are meant to occupy users' time, colonising local contexts and practices. One way this occurs is by making users angry at other people, or rather by encouraging them to seek out and become angered by other individuals. Consider journalistic practices of sharing "hot takes" or making use of "clickbait" titles to attract an emotionally invested readership (Ferrucci, 2022, pp. 2064, 2076).

Moreover, some loosely affiliated people linked to these venues also serve in governing these practices. Moderators (mods) and administrators (admins) are a human interface between individuals and platforms. They not only regulate relationships between individuals and other individuals by encouraging or discouraging a pile-on against a person, but may also serve as the 'face' of a platform. This reflects a broader tendency for platforms to deputise other users to serve as customer support.[3] Thus, even the boundary between platform and user is complicated by mods and admins, as platforms can offload large parts of their maintenance onto deputised and in some cases prominent users. While this chapter focuses on media platforms themselves, the liminal role moderators occupy between platforms and other users warrants further attention.

This chapter offers an exploratory and non-exhaustive overview of the media landscape that sustains the court of public opinion. The global digital media landscape of course features social media platforms, yet we also include legacy media that are also active on and beyond social media. Despite coping with diminished ad revenue and a crisis of legitimacy (McChesney, 2012), the press remain an influential source for making sense of new technology, new tech practices and new tech problems that are often framed as moral panics. As with the state, they are not the sole actors that summon an online mob or launch the court of public opinion. Rather, tabloids and other branches of the press are skilled at amplifying online shitstorms, and then benefiting from the fallout. When talking about 'the media,' social media platforms and the press are similar in their curation and distribution of information, including personal information about people, to a digitally accessible audience who are also solicited for commentary that is then published. In reconciling user empowerment with powerful platforms, we acknowledge that cases of mediated shaming and related practices are very much 'user-led.' Yet that does not exclude the fact that they are also governed by platforms that benefit from this activity. Mediated denunciations are an assembled process that can cast attention on specific targets and perpetrators, while entire industries profit from this activity. Media platforms distribute content, playing a pivotal role in making them meaningful. While it is tempting to otherwise distinguish social media from the press in terms of hosting user-generated content, it is important to also acknowledge how they co-produce mediated shaming.

We are left speculating about the extent to which mediated shaming practices are coordinated 'from above' by platforms and the press. User-led shaming is seemingly decoupled from state activity (although we problematise this claim in the next chapter), while dependent on some form of media platform to be visible and thus impactful. This chapter advances an understanding of how the 'reputation economy' (the public standing of people) and 'engagement economy' (the ability to mobilise people) coexist in a hybrid media ecosystem (Chadwick, 2017) where the press and platforms exploit the former to advance the latter.

Reputation as consumed in an engagement economy

User denunciation of other individuals is a means for platforms to generate audiences through engagement with both peers and prominent content creators. This engagement depends on voluntary and involuntary social exposure. Not only because cases involve people consenting and not consenting to participation, but also because consenting to some exposure can easily facilitate other instances of involuntary exposure. As seen in Chapter 3, prominent users gain followers as a form of capital, but also as a source of vulnerability. For platform owners, user visibility is a source of capital without being a vulnerability to the same existential degree.

Platforms are engines of an engagement economy, as advertising, data scraping and other forms of exploitation are predicated on users coming to these spaces. The engagement economy refers to the drive and mandate of business models in the media that are predicated on getting users to perform actions (Ørmen & Gregersen, 2023). User engagement is typically presented as a set of metrics for media businesses, including digital platforms and legacy press. But engagement – the ability to compel and mobilise others – is also an indicator that influencers and individuals in the job market must factor into their own professional planning. Tangible forms of user engagement include creating user-generated content and participating in viral campaigns. Yet more pervasive ones like comments and sharing can also count as engagement. Simply paying attention to a Twitter feed can be understood as a form of engagement,[4] as scrolling, clicking and cursor tracking are quantified metrics. All these tasks help retain users on platforms, enable the collection of their data and feed metrics that render these platforms profitable.

Alongside the engagement economy, individual reputation is exposed as a form of capital and concern for people, prominent or otherwise. As seen in Chapter 1 it is a way to assess and even quantify a person's public standing. There are many ways to measure reputation, and individuals are increasingly aware that their public standing can be tanked by an online shitstorm. Consider how high-profile examples of public shaming are processed through a lens of speculative job market advice.[5] Users may feel a need to be cautious and strategic in curating their personal image in public. Moreover, these cautious practices typically happen through the media, an obvious fact that should not be overlooked. Some researchers see dispersed reputation mechanisms as an infrastructure to scale up, by "leveraging our limited and local human judgement power with collective networked filtering" in order to "promote an interconnected ecology of socially beneficial reputation systems – to restrain the baser side of human nature, while unleashing positive social changes and enabling the realization of ever higher goals." (Masum & Zhang, 2004). Readers can recognise social benefits from enforced reputation harm. Public denunciations can be a useful and necessary social function to limit otherwise unsanctioned forms of abuse (Gajjala, 2018). Our concern in this chapter is when attacks on one's social standing are used in potentially harmful ways as part of media business models.

Scholars like Hearn (2010, p. 421) illuminate the reputation economy as shaped by political economic conditions, noting that "these practices herald a form of market discipline and affective conditioning." While celebrated as a form of "true transparency," (ibid., p. 430)

> [o]nline reputation measurement and management systems are new sites of cultural production; they are places where the expression of feeling is ostensibly constituted as 'reputation' and then mined for value. But, where, and for whom, are profits actually made in these processes?
>
> (ibid., p. 422)

Hearn provides an account of the kinds of actors making a business model out of online self-expression, at the time of the Web 2.0 uptake. Followings, connections and exposure amount to a set of means through which a person can make themselves known to the public. We arguably see an expansion of concern from an industry-oriented focus on the reputations of brands and companies, to the consumption of individual reputations as a more predominant mechanism for brand and broader organisational advancement. Langlois and Slane (2017, p. 120) examine pervasive "revenge porn"' economies, including websites like *MyEx.com*. Revenge porn is typically a gendered form of shaming that has become a routinised form of harm to those targeted, as well as a means for certain digital media 'entrepreneurs' to accrue wealth through violations of targeted women's privacy. Both offence- and defence-based management of reputation are monetised. Prominent antivirus software company Norton released *Reputation Defender* services as a range of "solutions" for businesses, "VIPs" and "personal branding."[6] They also claim to help clients manage review data, which is not only tangentially connected to individuals' reputations in the case of personal brands and larger enterprises (Welch, 2020), but also a growing domain for interpersonal and cultural grievances (Giacomo Cantone et al., 2021).

New initiatives by media companies (and other companies using media) attempt to tap into a type of public opinion. Expressed as "general sentiment" (Arvidsson & Peitersen, 2013; see also Hearn, 2010, p. 429), social media are sites for new practices to manage social relations. Since 2010 we have seen these new protocols continuously re-shaped, as when Reddit introduced the *Am I The Asshole* community, where users seek out moral judgement of incidents in which they were involved (Botzer et al., 2022). Engagement economies compel people to use digital media to generate feedback and evaluations about employees and members of a general public, in turn driving grievances to public and heavily promoted venues. Due to the popularity of platforms like Facebook and Reddit, this has become common knowledge to most casual users. Posting, scrubbing, finding and reporting 'problematic' content are controversial media practices that are heavily embedded in everyday media use.

Ultimately, engagement economy media practices like solicited reviews by third-party platforms can come at the expense of an individual's reputation. Returning to our understanding of reputation in Chapter 1, engagement economies operate through one understanding of reputation: word of mouth as an enabling and descriptive infrastructure (*getting people to talk about you*). This contrasts with a second understanding of reputation: word of mouth as normative and problematising content (*what they're saying about you isn't good*). The first understanding of reputation corresponds to generating prominence in the short term, and may endanger the second understanding of maintaining positive favour and not becoming a liability in the long term. Brighenti (2007) recognises how those dependent on platforms experience mediated visibility as empowering and disempowering, for instance in how celebrities cope with a tension between a need to maintain current relevance through a stream of fresh content, and maintaining positive recognition in the long term. Some public figures maintain their degree of relevance, yet most eventually fall from the upper stratum. Whether public-facing as a celebrity or in the service sector employee, ubiquitous reviewing practices are solicited by both organisations and mediating platforms. These reviews contribute to public opinion about the target, and grievances against them may culminate in a way that eventually harms their career prospects. For those targeted by negative reviews, there is also a clash between the reviewing platform's viability and their own reputation, especially in contexts where a drop from a perfect score (e.g. anything less than five stars on Uber) harms employees' success due to human and algorithmic sorting practices (Jamil, 2020).

On media venues that compel people to disclose personal details, and thus perform an 'authentic' self, this can amount to feeling the need to make potentially stigmatising disclosures to maintain high social media metrics and clout. Scholars should be attentive to histories of engagement-versus-reputation struggles across cultural contexts. Scrutiny and denunciation of public and marginally public figures are also seen in earlier media practices, including self-branding. Reality television programmes are a recent predecessor to peer scrutiny (Andrejevic, 2004) and suggest that provoking and mobilising people is a long-profitable cultural practice. These shows cultivate audiences that watch participants carefully for missteps and use digital platforms to denounce and downgrade their status. Most reality television formats share a focus on otherwise private individuals made public, typically scrutinised in a moral frame. This is most apparent in crime-based (Doyle, 2003) ones, but similar overtones are found in cohabitation and even makeover programmes (Marwick, 2010). Makeover shows in which people or their living spaces are revamped seek to 'get to the bottom' of a problem, typically with pre-existing frames of suspicion that expect a certain type of person beneath their artifice. As a media format, reality television generally fits an engagement economy, as the moral failings of others not only capture the attention of a loyal audience but also compel that audience to discuss online, create reaction videos and podcasts as well as generate other forms of content in response to these programmes (cf. Holmes, 2004).

We also see this tension between engagement and reputation in earlier iterations of the internet, for instance in Solove's (2007) examples of Web 1.0 sites that compel visitors to identify and denounce terrible people. These cases make up a fragmented and iterative web. They were associated with an internet that was less globally integrated into daily life, and did not command the same user base as today. Mediated shaming as a business model is not new, as we can locate an extensive history of platforms serving to get individuals to scrutinise and denounce other people, at the cost of their general public standing. Such groups are now housed on Facebook pages, subreddits and Twitter accounts. Vitriol, doxing and hate speech pervade, yet any community that embraces these may be living on borrowed time.

Coping with – and depending upon – volatile platforms

Below we unpack how digital media users make sense of scrutiny and denunciation on digital media platforms. This includes examining the role and function of platforms and other media services. Underlying these discussions are concerns about who has control over these spaces, and how someone can work ethically in and through these spaces. Finally, we consider what changes are necessary to minimise the harms that our respondents identify.

Relations between individuals and digital media can be fundamentally troubling for respondents, due to their dependence on volatile platforms. Respondents identify engagement as a driving force online, which involves being visible and making others visible in order to provoke reactions from an audience. This is how platforms are valued and monetised, but also how many public-facing individuals are expected to successfully operate on social media. A media designer in the Netherlands believes YouTube works with the logic that any engagement is good engagement, such that "bad publicity becomes good publicity on YouTube," noting that even gestures that signal disapproval like the "thumbs down" generate "the same revenue (…). It's engagement anyway. So engagement really doesn't see if you're enjoying it or not. You're just watching the movie." In cultivating engagement that "doesn't pick sides," platform operators act as information brokers, or rather as mercenaries in all-pervasive culture wars (Proctor & Kies, 2018). Thus, the public relations claim that 'any publicity is good publicity' seems to apply more to the platform itself, rather than to the individual or brand that navigates the platform and faces the negative consequences of the outrage.

Platforms and users become joint beneficiaries of engagement when users can monetise this activity. Yet monetisation is difficult for individuals to attain, and losing engagement can endanger their labour. A software developer from the UK notes the difficulty in getting people to notice their social initiatives and stay engaged, especially when that involves having followers generate content. In the context of citizen science, he states that "all of our projects suffer with this" and that "even if you manage to attract people to the project, even if you manage to get them to hear about it somehow, which is no mean feat in this very busy, crowded technological environment (…) how do you keep them engaged with it?" He goes on to describe losing engagement from digital media users as "the perennial problem that we face," especially for new and fledgling initiatives.

The perceived requirement to be online is presented as almost existential, certainly for businesses, or anyone dependent on some kind of market. A Canadian journalist reflects on the kinds of media literacy that are necessary to "be effective" on digital platforms, in the context of union organisers, activists and others who may court controversy: "Not everyone has the same level of literacy. Not everyone's literacy is built around a platform like Twitter," notably if they generate content that ends up being mismatched with the venue and received as "really long essays." Such practices signal being "total shit at Twitter" which becomes "a huge problem" for users. She goes on to clarify that the "mitigating factor between your actions and how someone's receiving your actions" is not a public service, but rather a "for-profit platform. And we've rendered it invisible, but it's not. It's still there. I mean, we're always speaking through a for-profit platform. And we don't talk about that." The denunciations and vitriolic exchanges that take place through Twitter end up obscuring how these platforms benefit from cultivating and promoting social discord. Since this interview took place Twitter was acquired by Elon Musk, a polarising figure who drew negative attention to the platform while making it less accessible to the general public.[7] Yet a significant amount of public denunciation of Twitter and its owner continues to take place on Twitter, which speaks to how embedded it is in public discourse. Respondents refer to the internet not as a diverse range of options, but rather as a consolidated set of powerful sites. This in turn contributes to an asymmetry of power relations between major media platforms and everyone else who seems to depend on them. An American data scientist states that she "lament[s] the death of the internet because I think that we don't really have an internet anymore. We have like five websites and that's it." She identifies this loss as a motivation for a lot of her projects, in seeking to "recreate a little bit of that old energy that it had." This is a considerable challenge, even for someone with her skills and devotion, and she positions this ambition within a "trend of like wanting to go back to blogging, wanting to go back to long-form journalism and wanting to go back to, like, and building websites and like, you know, getting away from Twitter, Facebook, Google, YouTube and Amazon."

Digital media platforms are volatile, and respondents reflect on how user practices change over time. A media professional in the Netherlands notes her mercurial relation with Twitter's API, such that current practices to gather information from the platform have a limited shelf life. In terms of social know-how, a Dutch filmmaker notes how young people seem to be more comfortable with the internet, which reflects a generation shift that older users struggle with. Cultural gaps between generations go hand in hand with steep learning curves for new platforms. Engagement is both a matter of tech-savvy and cultural relevance. She describes this learning curve when receiving guidance for curating personal content from youth in the context of an earlier project. These young girls informed her that she "had too many drunk photos on Facebook." This exchange was an indication of how "young people are also getting more used to the internet and the rules of the internet. And because I didn't have that as a child (…) I never learned about that." Despite the youth being better prepared for life on the internet, she adds that this does not translate to more civil behaviour towards their peers: "when I asked the children now how they bully or maybe shame each other online, they told me with stickers." Young users instead adapt their incivility to new platform features like affixing digital "stickers" to photos of targeted peers.

Inclusion and exclusion from platforms

The above struggles shape users' sense of belonging to – and exclusion from – social platforms. The press historically hold a clear social purpose when they are rooted in a region and make appeals to those who identify with that territory. These appeals include us-versus-them narratives about those who breach social norms (Clark, 2015), in turn reproducing a sense of belonging and exclusion. Yet we can consider how social media users position themselves within platforms that compel people to be present and cultivate scrutiny and denunciation against others. For a UK-based journalist, the geographic perception users hold of platforms matters. As seen in Chapter 2, she was photographed and confronted by a Facebook group meant to shame people from a separate continent. Upon discovering that the group seemed to be confined to a different part of the world, she was less concerned with the potential for social sanction. Both geography, demographics and platform choice mattered, as she believes Twitter posts are more likely to go viral in a way that transcends local contexts:

> [T]he potential for things to totally go viral on Twitter is quite high. But my conception of Facebook, because it's something that I know, like young people don't sit scrolling on Facebook, I was like, this is (…) for more middle-aged Australians of whom I know nothing.

Here a combination of perceived understandings of age, location and platform use makes her potential denunciation on this space a less tangible threat to her well-being.

Beyond international social media sites, Dutch respondents repeatedly identify local platforms as having a national presence and persistence. The filmmaker characterised the media-sharing platform *Dumpert* in terms of a moral ambivalence of justice and abuse, in response to the negative reputation it otherwise cultivates. She acknowledges that she is "shaming *Dumpert* but they also screen nice stuff, like kid's things." She generalises this ambivalence by noting "that's also how the internet works [...] if you've done something really nicely or really beautifully, it ends up on the internet as well." Platforms like *Dumpert* – or YouTube or Twitter – make appeals to their audience through emotions like anger and revulsion, but also less problematic ones. She processes this tension by outlining the appeal of *Dumpert* as curating the best media content in a localised setting, noting that its branding is derived from the local community it evokes as a result. This community is sustained from the efforts of its user base: "in the Netherlands there are all videos of people who shot themselves or just saw something on the street and they send it to *Dumpert* themselves." Not only is this local mobilisation a source of engagement, but platforms like *Dumpert* and its affiliated site *GeenStijl* [Tasteless] are "powerful" because they are able to mobilise user vitriol against targets without making themselves immediately visible, a feature she likens to throwing feces from a sheltered position: "they are never talking. It's like [hiding behind] a wall, throwing shit over it. You cannot do something with them." This elaboration points to a condition where the owners of the platform are understood as not speaking directly, and thus not making themselves subject to scrutiny. She goes on to liken them to "a big army," adding that they are "making a sport out of" engaging with targeted people, and mobilising a loyal user base against these targets. She also notes that describing *Dumpert* and *Geenstijl* as a social force also seems ambivalent as "it's more a feeling that they are really powerful (...) in the end, it's just comments." Respondents struggle to conceptualise the kind of influence social media communities have in denouncing targets, whether they ruin lives or "just" produce comments.

A Dutch media professional was targeted by *GeenStijl* and *Dumpert* when she made a politicised statement in a national newspaper. When she discovered this, she struggled to determine how to respond. Her colleagues advised her against reading "all the comments" beneath the denunciatory post. She did so anyway, partly out of curiosity "from a psychological point of view" but also admitted that she "wasn't prepared" for the extent of their vitriol. A Dutch knowledge worker also faced online shaming on *Dumpert*, and feared that asking the site to take down content may make it worse: "and now I'm still in doubt whether I'm going to contact them to take it down because I'm afraid they might misuse my mail." For this reason, she believes it is preferable to ignore online activity and attempt to hide from such attacks, if possible.

When seeking alternatives to global platforms based in Silicon Valley, 'local' is not necessarily an improvement for residents of that space. Such a platform may pride itself on being independent from outside influence, but may be in a greater position to not only bring harm to targets in their own region, but may even cultivate their own localised communities based on these practices. Local torment is also experienced with the press. An academic based in the Netherlands experienced how an employer may harm its own workers in seeking to appease a journalist network: "they're prepared to throw staff and students under the bus in order to (…) perceived to be okay by the people who shout very loudly from the alt-right in Dutch media." She states her frustration with "the fact that the university is supposed to be scared of a few petulant middle aged white dudes who seem to dominate the media landscape in the Netherlands." By identifying "a few petulant middle aged white dudes" as the prominent face of a hostile local mediascape, she offers an account of the court of public opinion being led or at least swayed by recognisable faces of legacy media, in contrast to the attributing this influence to faceless online mobs.

Maintaining control and achieving consent

When navigating online exchanges, consent and control are ambivalent in practice. Not only do respondents feel compelled to work through digital platforms, but they also acknowledge that these bring certain affordances to communicate, including in ways that circumvent legacy media. The American data scientist sees social media as unfiltered through news giants like the Associated Press or *New York Times*, notably in the context of political protests at the time in Portland and Minneapolis. These allow media users "to get a more diverse and wide-ranging picture of what's happening." While respondents find themselves on these platforms as an implicit or explicit professional requirement, they also acknowledge potential benefits that are not possible with other major media platforms.

Loss of control over content is a theme that other respondents address. For the Dutch knowledge worker, once you upload content onto a platform "it's not under your control anymore, and it can lead a whole different life that you didn't intend to." The use of the term "life" here underscores the long-term trajectory of content that has been released onto global networks. A UK-based journalist also notes a loss of control upon posting and makes a link between sharing content and online gambling due to a perceived potential 'win' of engagement for users. She notes that users "don't actually ever know what response you're going to get so you can post in the form of people who you think might respond in a positive way, but they also might not. They might not see it." She sees this potential as a dimension of "losing control when you put information onto an online sphere." A user might have an intended outcome when posting, such as reaching and mobilising a relevant network of like-minded peers. Not only might this not happen, such that those peers "might not see it," but at a later point in time a less sympathetic user base may take this content out of context, and use it against the user, or a vulnerable community they represent. In reflecting on this loss of control across contexts, this respondent states that she doesn't "know if everyone who posts on Facebook or Twitter like Instagram instantly thinks like I've lost control of this information, but you kind of have and you don't really get to set the way that it's perceived after that." This speaks to how this loss of control is an often-unspoken element of posting that warrants greater attention from users, especially those who consider themselves "kind of control obsessed."

The Dutch filmmaker also reflects on the role of consent in her own practice, namely towards those she features in her movies. When making media content on online grievances, obtaining consent is a sensitive process, because it brings a public exposition of a low point in the consenting person's life. When the goal is to convey someone else's lived experience, not only might this fail, but it might bring additional harm to the person who entrusted a media actor with their time and reputation. She speculates whether it is possible or truly desirable to tell another person's story,[8] reflecting on an individual who was publicly shamed, and how he was willing to work with her: "they wanted to share their story (…) because they felt like they couldn't tell their version of the story" through social media platforms or the press. This respondent went on to reflect on how she might have failed to live up to this promise:

> Even now when I'm telling this, I'm like, I never told his whole story in the film. So (…) I did the same thing maybe in the film. He's in the film. He ended up in the film because he was the person who's telling the audience how big the consequences are. But I didn't tell his story.

If lack of control over one's public narrative is a perceived harm in media shaming, attempts to evoke sympathy and understanding of these targets may also fail to empower these targets. Despite this admission, she also acknowledges that content creators like herself cope with a relative lack of control in a broader national media network, namely in terms of how their content is framed and delivered to an audience. Content producers are ultimately subservient to those who oversee channels, including those marketing content to audiences through these channels.

Revisiting digital media ethics

Respondents also reflect on how their experiences on media platforms have led them to change their behaviour online, as well as how these reflections shape their views on the ethics of digital media. The UK-based journalist states that following her own experience with online shaming, she would not write articles that exploit social media outrage, especially taking potentially offensive content out of context, in contrast with most tabloids: "there's a certain type of article and writing which is like sort of crowdsourcing something viral on the internet and then just kind of writing about it, you know, being like 'the internet's going crazy at this woman.'" This parallels her revelation in Chapter 2 that she would not share image-based content about strangers in interpersonal communications, with a similar ethic applied to her professional content. She goes on to clarify that she previously felt an aversion to this kind of media content and "would not be interested in doing that anyway" but that her recent experiences with media shaming heightened her awareness of the harm it brings.

The academic, based in the Netherlands, reflects on the role of media, noting how media-borne outrage necessitates a "duty of care" towards members of the public. When she and her colleagues were targeted by digital media users, and this caught the attention of a politicised press, she was frustrated that:

> what was very obvious from most of the media inquiries was there was no interest in them having a duty of care towards me or my colleagues. They just wanted, again, the outrage. They wanted to magnify it for the clicks, for the revenue. They had no interest in a nuanced discussion.

She also reflects on the ethics of not publishing something terrible yet marketable, noting that the current media landscape means that outrage "gets amplified in a way that it has a reach that it didn't have before," and that "there are certain people that can take responsibility for amplifying it." While the internet appears to play a role in shitstorms, she notes "when you're a large international publishing house and you choose to give people a book deal. On the basis of that, the outrageous and contrary, whatever stuff that they say on the internet, then you have to take responsibility for it." An ethical intervention here would be contemplating the possibility that "we don't have to publish this" rather than "generating a profit off of that." The Dutch knowledge worker acknowledges media platforms' dependence on advertising, which means abandoning a sense of social responsibility: "And this is the business. News media is a business. Yeah. Advertisers are using *Dumpert* to reach their audience, but yeah. So I feel this is not corporate responsible behavior. Definitely not."

Recommendations for a safer media landscape

Having experienced and witnessed abuse and exploitation through digital platforms, digital media users we spoke to had recommendations for remedying social harms related to these platforms. A media designer based in the Netherlands notes that eventually "big mainstream social media" will have to "make a stand" with regard to the content and activity they host and support: "I know that they want to please everyone because it's what's better for the business. But in the future, I think they will have to make a stand." In straightforward terms, an academic also based in the Netherlands recommends that platforms like Twitter could "do a better job of getting rid of fascists." She notes that while reporting functions are already in place, "reporting can also be done maliciously, right? Yeah. Like all of these things, everything has multiple uses, but I think they could take the problem more seriously." In other words, tech-based solutions risk being ineffective or counterproductive if they are integrated without proper oversight.[9]

Beyond taking a stand against fascists, respondents like the media designer based in the Netherlands also describe digital media reform in terms of "a lot of small stuff." Some of this amounts to greater transparency of platform functioning to the public, such as knowing "if you are speaking with a bot or with a person" when engaging with Twitter. She also frames her recommendations in terms of her background as a graphic designer, noting that platforms play a crucial role in shaping user practices, and that these technical aspects "can be more down to earth." She gives the example of comment sections prompting users to "write your own story," or implementing a "cooling off" period before successive postings, as ways of re-centring human actors in potentially abusive communicative practices. She also notes that platform architecture "already influences us in so many ways" that they ought to consider applying these forms of manipulation for socially beneficial ends. Platform design choices can curb or dampen harmful excess of user input in public denunciations. Design-conscious platforms may limit public exposure and outrage, yet as social interfaces users experience them as "sterile" and less engaging by failing to account for their socio-affective needs. The UK-based software developer frames denunciation as communal and therapeutic, noting how platforms like apps struggle to fulfil these functions:

> You want to say to someone this is a problem and have some sort of social validation in terms of other people saying, 'oh, yeah, it's really horrible, we need to do something about that.' And actually, apps are very sterile in that sense that you're not really talking to a person. Okay, you're submitting a record, you're getting some degree of feedback, but you're not really getting that social or social validation. You're not getting someone patting you on the shoulder and saying, yeah, this is horrible. Let's do something about this. There isn't that sort of 'I'm part of a community.' And you can try to get that in a software product, but you'll never really achieve it in the same way that you would from a therapy group where people go and sit around and sort of bang their fists or, hug each other and say, yes. You know, we all feel the same.

The problems at hand are bigger than any single platform. The academic based in the Netherlands acknowledges that we must take a societal approach that accounts for local digital media users' choices, as well as the education system that did not adequately prepare their critical thinking. While noting that Facebook played a pivotal role in the Cambridge Analytica scandal and Brexit, and should indeed be held accountable, she also notes "it's not enough just to blame Facebook or Cambridge Analytica (…) it's also way bigger than that. It's a failure of the British education system to teach people critical thinking skills to weigh up and assess different forms of evidence." The Dutch filmmaker extends this sense of being complicit in media shaming by including her own role: "because I'm watching those videos, because they're ending up on my Facebook page, I'm part of the system as well, because I'm giving the view." When attributing social harm to digital platforms, it remains important to acknowledge the role of other social actors, including educators and users themselves, in either cultivating or performing harmful practices like doxing or hate speech.

Other respondents also go beyond platforms to consider other relations between individuals and public data. The American data scientist specifies a need for increased "open access to public records and to court records, reducing the barriers to freedom of information requests, things like that." This need is based on the diminished resources of viable media alternatives, such as local press that may only have a handful of "reporters on their normal beat" and thus "don't have time to do the deep dive investigations citizens do." Reporting on social issues, in the name of public interest, should ideally become media practices with low barriers to entry. When it comes to digital media platforms' role in reporting, a Canadian journalist notes that social media platforms are "destroying local news," and wants platforms to stop exploiting people involved in personal tragedies. She regards government regulation as a viable response to the current situation where "there's a lot of people that make a lot of money off of how exploitable [tragic events] are." State regulation suggests a more explicit recognition by governments of serial reputational harm as a reason for social media platforms "to be reined in." A lack of financing is an obstacle to socially healthy media practice, according to the UK software developer: "we can probably do everything that we want to, but it's very, very expensive."

Conclusion

Press and digital platforms shape public opinion, including about public opinion itself. Not only do they play a pivotal role in determining individual reputation, but also shape how the public thinks about these forms of normative and moral policing. This informs research on mediated shaming by shedding light on the tensions and harms media users experience because of how platforms direct negative attention and sentiment to others. Our respondents are ambivalent about digital media's potential for healthy social relations. The academic based in the Netherlands notes the possibility of nuance on platforms like Twitter, adding that she uses social media "with the intention of either trying to nuance the debate" and "give voice or give power or support or solidarity to people whose voices are marginalized." Yet despite this potential, other respondents do not have much faith in the internet becoming less toxic, or platforms like Twitter implementing reforms. The American essayist cites the lack of face-to-face interaction as well as platforms' profit motives as reasons not to expect a better outcome:

> [I]t's just almost like putting everyone in this real anonymity where they're just like a punching bag instead of a person. So I just don't have that much faith for the internet's ability to kind of mature in that way. And I think social media platforms like Twitter don't have the interest for that either, you know, because this is getting more people on Twitter, more people on social media, even if it's a toxic person.

Distilling the social benefits from these clear downsides, respondents like the software engineer note that social media teach us "that people desperately want their stories told. So let's pair them with the storytellers to make that happen." People value storytelling, including as a means for validation. We interpret storytelling to mean crafting a narrative, through the selective and strategic amplification of voices. Social media are the most accessible outlet for storytelling, and this often amounts to generating reputational harm in order to engage audiences. Co-operative models are recommended as courts of public opinion (cf. Fuchs, 2010). There are already less toxic examples for social interaction online (Yu et al., 2020), but they may not be scalable to the same degree as Facebook or YouTube, especially if they compete with global platforms like Meta and Google.

Digital platforms and the press largely shape how people punish each other, and these specific features need to be carefully designed and regulated. The most effective approach would be for platforms to get their audiences to refrain from engaging with potentially viral content that features a person being targeted. This is of course at cross-purposes with their business models, such that state regulation may need to mitigate platform exploitation of personal reputation. While police and politicians can oversee and mitigate harm, they are also poised to exploit digital shaming fervour, for instance as a form of populist mobilisation. The next chapter addresses state participation in mediated shaming practices more broadly.

Notes

1 https://knowyourmeme.com/photos/1862952-twitter-x. See for example https://twitter.com/dril/status/1035218616403128320

2 https://x.com/maplecocaine/status/1080665226410889217. See also https://knowyourmeme.com/memes/twitters-main-character

3 See for example Apple's "Support Community," where users can "[c]onnect with Apple customers around the world" to "[f]ind answers": https://discussions.apple.com/welcome

4 As concepts, attention and engagement economies largely overlap, and are often treated as synonymous in scholarly and trade literature. To distinguish the two, an attention economy without active user-led engagement can be understood as lurking, or listening (Crawford, 2009). An attention economy by itself is a less visible user practice that matters for the purposes of growing accustomed to watching others (Andrejevic, 2004) and normalising themselves being visible on platforms in non-visible ways.

5 https://www.forbes.com/sites/jeffbercovici/2013/12/23/justine-sacco-and-the-self-inflicted-perils-of-twitter/

6 https://www.reputationdefender.com/
7 https://inews.co.uk/news/technology/elon-musk-emergency-tweet-rationing-bad-future-decaying-dysfunctional-twitter-2448538
8 This is a question we also consider in empirical research on media shaming, which informs our decision to anonymise many cases as well as pseudonymise interviewees.
9 https://www.theverge.com/2014/9/2/6083647/facebook-s-report-abuse-button-has-become-a-tool-of-global-oppression (from Hintz, 2016).

References

Andrejevic, M. (2004). *Reality TV: The work of being watched.* Rowman & Littlefield Publishers.

Arvidsson, A., & Peitersen, N. (2013). *The ethical economy*. Columbia University Press.

Bakker, P. (2012). Aggregation, content farms and Huffinization: The rise of low-pay and no-pay journalism. *Journalism Practice*, *6*(5–6), 627–637. https://doi.org/10.1080/17512786.2012.667266

Botzer, N., Gu, S., & Weninger, T. (2022). Analysis of moral judgment on Reddit. *IEEE Transactions on Computational Social Systems*, *10*(3), 947–957. https://doi.org/10.1109/tcss.2022.3160677

Brighenti, A. (2007). Visibility: A category for the social sciences. *Current Sociology*, *55*(3), 323–342. https://doi.org/10.1177/0011392107076079

Chadwick, A. (2017). *The hybrid media system: Politics and power*. Oxford University Press. https://doi.org/10.1093/oso/9780190696726.001.0001

Clark, C. (2015). Integration, exclusion and the moral 'othering' of Roma migrant communities in Britain. In M. Smith (Ed.), *Moral regulation*(pp. 43–56). Policy Press. https://doi.org/10.56687/9781447366782-007

Clarke, R. (2014). The prospects for consumer-oriented social media. *Organizacija*, *47*(4), 291–230. https://doi.org/10.2478/orga-2014-0024

Crawford, K. (2009). Following you: Disciplines of listening in social media. *Continuum*, *23*(4), 525–535. https://doi.org/10.1080/10304310903003270

Doyle, A. (2003). *Arresting images: Crime and policing in front of the television camera*. University of Toronto Press. https://doi.org/10.3138/9781442671003

Ferrucci, P. (2022). Joining the team: Metajournalistic discourse, paradigm repair, the athletic and sports journalism practice. *Journalism Practice*, *16*(10), 2064–2082. https://doi.org/10.1080/17512786.2021.1907213

Foos, F., & Bischof, D. (2022). Tabloid media campaigns and public opinion: Quasi-experimental evidence on Euroscepticism in England. *American Political Science Review*, *116*(1), 19–37. https://doi.org/10.1017/s000305542100085x

Fuchs, C. (2010). Theoretical foundations of defining the participatory, co-operative, sustainable information society. *Information, Communication & Society*, *13*(1), 23–47. https://doi.org/10.1080/13691180902801585

Gajjala, R. (2018). When an Indian whisper network went digital. *Communication Culture & Critique*, *11*(3), 489–493. https://doi.org/10.1093/ccc/tcy025

Giacomo Cantone, G, Tomaselli, V., & Mazzeo, V. (2021). Ideology-driven polarisation in online ratings: The review bombing of The Last of Us Part II. *arXiv e-prints*. https://doi.org/10.48550/arXiv.2104.01140

Hearn, A. (2010). Structuring feeling: Web 2.0, online ranking and rating, and the digital 'reputation' economy. *Ephemera: Theory & Politics in Organization*, *10*(3/4), 421–438.

Hesmondhalgh, D. (2010). User-generated content, free labour and the cultural industries. *Ephemera*, 10(3/4), 267–284.

Hintz, A. (2016). Restricting digital sites of dissent: Commercial social media and free expression. *Critical Discourse Studies*, *13*(3), 325–340.

Holmes, S. (2004). 'But this time you choose!' Approaching the 'interactive' audience in reality tv. *International Journal of Cultural Studies*, *7*(2), 213–231. https://doi.org/10.1177/1367877904043238

Jamil, R. (2020). Uber and the making of an Algopticon: Insights from the daily life of Montreal drivers. *Capital & Class*, *44*(2), 241–260. https://doi.org/10.2139/ssrn.3490030

Langlois, G., & Slane, A. (2017). Economies of reputation: The case of revenge porn. *Communication and Critical/Cultural Studies*, *14*(2), 120–138. https://doi.org/10.1080/14791420.2016.1273534

Lawrence, R. G., & Bennett, W. L. (2001). Rethinking media politics and public opinion: Reactions to the Clinton-Lewinsky scandal. *Political Science Quarterly*, *116*(3), 425–446. https://doi.org/10.2307/798024

Marwick, A. (2010). There's a beautiful girl under all of this: Performing hegemonic femininity in reality television. *Critical Studies in Media Communication*, *27*(3), 251–266. https://doi.org/10.1080/15295030903583515

Masum, H., & Zhang, Y. (2004). Manifesto for the reputation society. *First Monday*, *9*(7). https://doi.org/10.5210/fm.v9i7.1158

McChesney, R. W. (2012). Farewell to journalism? Time for a rethinking. *Journalism Practice*, *6*(5–6), 614–626. https://doi.org/10.1080/17512786.2012.683273

Ørmen, J., & Gregersen, A. (2023). Towards the engagement economy: Interconnected processes of commodification on YouTube. *Media, Culture & Society*, *45*(2), 225–245. https://doi.org/10.1177/01634437221111951

Proctor, W., & Kies, B. (2018). On toxic fan practices and the new culture wars. *Participations*, *15*(1), 127–142.

Solove, D. J. (2007).*The future of reputation: Gossip, rumor, and privacy on the internet.* Yale University Press. https://doi.org/10.12987/9780300138191

Trottier, D. (2020). Confronting the digital mob: Press coverage of online justice seeking. *European Journal of Communication*, *35*(6), 597–612. https://doi.org/10.1177/0267323120928234

Trottier, D., Huang, Q., & Gabdulhakov, R. (2021). Covidiots as global acceleration of local surveillance practices. *Surveillance & Society*, *19*(1), 109–113. https://doi.org/10.24908/ss.v19i1.14546

Welch, J. (2020). What's in a name? Complications in overcoming reputational damage during the corporate recovery process. *Strategic Direction*, *36*(3), 1–3. https://doi.org/10.1108/sd-09-2019-0167

Yu, B., Seering, J., Spiel, K., & Watts, L. (2020, April). "Taking care of a fruit tree": Nurturing as a layer of concern in online community moderation. In*Extended Abstracts of the 2020 CHI Conference on Human Factors in Computing Systems*. April, 1–9. https://doi.org/10.1145/3334480.3383009

5 The role of states

Police, polarisation and populism

Less doxing, more tip lines?

States take diverse approaches in response to people denouncing each other. In 2021, the Dutch government moved to outlaw doxing,[1] thus asserting control over whether people can publish other people's personal information. States are often seen as lagging in their response to emerging harmful user-led digital media practices, including cyberbullying (Goff, 2011). Anti-doxing legislation can be understood as catching up to the possibilities for reputational harm that digital media afford us. At the same time, Dutch politicians, among others, make appeals to the public for them to watch over and report their neighbours. In some cases, due to temporary public health measures.[2] In other cases, it is against indoctrination in the classroom.[3]

Varying state involvement in mediated shaming can also be observed in the UK and China, where the state instructed local platforms to regulate and manage doxing and online violence[4] after several high-profile cases of public denunciation led to targets' taking their own lives. Unlike the kinds of denunciation seen in previous chapters, many of these state-led initiatives handle data about targeted suspects as confidential. By using secure tip lines instead of public fora, neither the target nor the person lodging the complaint will necessarily become a target of public scrutiny. Such claims rest on the assumption that sensitive information remains confidential, while leaks are a persistent risk due to a combination of platform features and strategic media practice (cf. Lyon, 2001). When states encourage digital media users to denounce peers and neighbours via secure government channels, these users may feel emboldened to condemn the same target through a panoply of local and global fora. Someone compelled to denounce their neighbour to an anonymous hotline may also share this information with a neighbourhood WhatsApp group, or local Reddit or Facebook group. In the Netherlands, some *Buurtpreventie* [neighbourhood watch] WhatsApp groups voluntarily report perceived suspicious actions or intruders in the neighbourhood. Similarly, Chinese WeChat community groups coordinated contact tracing and testing during the pandemic, and enforced public health measures including neighbourhood lockdowns (Liu et al., 2023). Some of these denunciations have been framed as

DOI: 10.4324/9781003453017-5

civic engagement or participation (cf. Barney et al., 2016). We can identify characteristics that distinguish desirable from socially damaging forms of civilian lateral scrutiny. Yet states along with media platforms may promote novel and disproportionate forms of civilian scrutiny and denunciation by framing it in terms of civic duty and patriotism. Other states actively repress problematic forms of civilian participation for more self-serving reasons. In Russia, recent interventions reflect a kind of authoritarian "gardening" (Litvinenko & Toepfl, 2019, p. 225), where branches of the state weed out inconvenient media and discourses that may otherwise reach local audiences.

States may seem to lose control over social sanction and punishment when informal shaming by civilians expands in frequency and reach through digital media. Local authorities will then trial new ways to mobilise individual scrutiny and reporting, in a perennial and iterative manner. This includes tip lines that encourage individuals to provide information about specific types of wrongdoings, such as the identity of the target and any evidence of their misdeeds. It also includes states soliciting shaming of civilians on digital media in novel ways that provoke multiple forms of engagement from digital media users, like when police in Maricopa County, Arizona oversaw a "Mugshot of the Day" website (Young, 2020, p. 307). States can also establish legal frameworks that nudge platforms and users to engage in mediated scrutiny and denunciation. As one example, by making platforms liable for distributing "harmful content," the Chinese government directs platforms to develop affordances and self-governance mechanisms where individual users are encouraged to report wrongdoings on social media platforms, such as posting vulgar and politically sensitive content.

Finally, states can lead public shaming by setting agendas on mainstream media by calling out certain groups or certain types of behaviour. This can be observed in Russia where amid the full-scale invasion of Ukraine, the state has divided the society into 'good' and 'bad' citizens: supporters and opponents of war, respectively. As a result, Soviet-era snitching culture has become widespread. The scope of 'bad' citizens is ever-expanding, as state media censor *Roskomnadzor* provides online submission forms for snitching reports on sexual minority content. After the Supreme Court deemed the "global LGBT movement" extremist in November 2023, the state began issuing fines and other sanctions for displaying rainbow colours in public.[5] In one instance, the punishment for wearing rainbow-coloured earrings went as far as five days of detainment. The woman in question was sitting with her friend in a cafe in Nizhny Novgorod when strangers approached them angrily and filmed themselves demanding the young man to remove a badge resembling the Ukrainian flag from his sweater. "Are you aware of the situation in the country?" one of the strangers asked, "Take that off now, bitch."[6] The vigilantes threatened to share their footage with Russia's "Centre E" (centre for combating extremism under the Ministry of Internal Affairs), and evidently did so. This case was the first detainment for displaying the "extremist" symbol, yet the story began with the Ukrainian flag and ended with the rainbow earrings that the woman happened to be wearing. The law in this case is vague and can be selectively applied to punish people for their political views.

These state initiatives emerge concurrently with citizens and civilians more broadly[7] recording, confronting and denouncing people they designate as a public safety risk (Lub, 2018) or as problematic in some other sense of the term. Given the broad range of offences that mobilise individuals, digitised courts of public opinion are processes that governments may wish to not only contain or suppress, but also, depending on the circumstances, stoke and direct. Vigilant audiences are at once an opportunity and a problem for states to manage. Individual politicians and political staffers can mobilise vigilant audiences to defame competitors or denounce critical journalists and dissidents. These audiences may be motivated by a sense of duty to the state, by contentious and often polarising politics or due to career advancement and other forms of self-interest. These motivations also compel states to sanction and censor user-led online shitstorms. This chapter unpacks promotional and repressive initiatives as attempts by states to wrest control of runaway social shaming and punishment from civilians.

Situating the state in the wake of (digital) vigilantism

States are typically understood as slow to react to developments involving digital media and active users. Yet we can observe police and other functions of the state adapting to an 'extremely online' populace. Miliband (1969, p. 47) cites Weber to approach states as bearing a "monopoly of legitimate use of physical force within a given territory." To this we can add an increased use of other kinds of violence, including cultural harm that target an individual or community's public standing (Galtung, 1990). In re-asserting control over sanction and harm, states can thus not only mobilise civilian-led embodied mobs, but also outsource a more totalising social sanction to a global media audience.

This chapter begins to account for the role of states in the court of public opinion. In seeking to reconcile state-led and civilian-led media shaming initiatives, we first acknowledge that state initiatives have porous boundaries with civilian media practice. A case of mediated shaming may be understood as civilian-led in its genesis, yet police may then co-opt the sentiment, the data, the participants and the platform.[8] Likewise, police may attempt to mobilise civilians to report on their peers, but this can easily go beyond what they would consider appropriate, lawful and proportionate.[9] To add to this complexity, 'the state' is composed of various actors situated in separate branches that may struggle with conflicting interests (cf. Miliband, 1969). In principle, law enforcement – the police – acts as the agent of the government and the interface between state interests and civilians. Therefore, the state and the police are often discussed interchangeably in academic writing and public discourse.

However, such alignment might not always be (perceived as) true, especially when the target is an individual police officer. For example, in 2017 a local police officer in China's Henan province was named and shamed on Sina Weibo due to his violence against civilians and involvement with local gang members. Yet the target was perceived as a "problematic individual police" in both public and media discourses and the case ended with an official punishment of the officer, as announced by the state oversight institution and state media.[10] This misalignment can also be observed in Western democracies where legislation, administration, judicial power and public media can all be understood as 'the state' while these components may disagree when it comes to handling public denunciation of targeted individuals.[11]

We approach relations between civilians and the state as multi-directional, mobilising a diverse range of political, civilian and media actors (Trottier & Fuchs, 2014). In taking an exploratory approach to state responses to the court of public opinion, we question whether a civilian-led movement can gain momentum without being appropriated in some form by states, or private actors for that matter. We often think in terms of a binary distinction between state-led and civilian-led vigilante justice. But this distinction has been complicated, as seen in historical examples of concerned individuals in Chapter 2, or when off-duty police officers would participate as KKK members in the US (Amann, 1983). In communist countries such as China, resident committees [居委会, *juweihui*] or communities [社区, *shequ*] are closely tied to the state apparatus and operate as an extension of the government, despite their grassroots appearance. Rather than fostering bottom-up participation, they primarily serve as tools for state control and surveillance by implementing state policies, monitoring civilians and managing social stability (Tomba, 2014). Thus, we maintain a conceptual distinction between state and non-state actors while addressing how they shape each other, specifically in response to opportunities and constraints that civilians, private media platforms and prevailing regimes bear upon each other.

Police are an exemplary component of the state, but we also consider a wider range of local authorities as well as public broadcasters and other state-led media venues. States embody civil services, but also party politics, such that an otherwise effective initiative from the 'wrong' political party may be attacked by opposing factions. The state is composed of dissenting, oppositional and potentially marginalised interests. In a parliamentary democracy, elected officials of a minority party with a few seats may not be able to claim that they act on behalf of 'the state,' especially if they are not part of the ruling government. Yet they remain representatives of the state, and can attempt to shape how individuals denounce and are denounced by each other. For instance, a Dutch far-right populist politician set up a hotline for locals to denounce Central and Eastern European labourers, in turn also provoking denunciations by elected officials and civilians against the hotline itself.[12]

In focusing on states managing and stoking online denunciations, we build on scholarship addressing earlier initiatives in which branches of the state call upon their population to report suspicious activities in both public and private spaces (Reeves, 2012, p. 235; Lippert & Wilkinson, 2010). These works rightly indicate that such initiatives not only pre-date a contemporary digital media landscape but are perennial methods for local authorities to extend their reach in policing criminal activity as well. In doing so, this scholarship highlights a continued reproduction of discrimination through these crowdsourcing efforts, especially when civilians make use of similarly vague criteria of 'suspicion' as law enforcement. What we address below extends from a primary focus on crime fighting to broader moral policing as well as political opportunism when establishing a common enemy by stoking moral panics. As seen in Chapter 1, state officials are themselves coping with and responding to being made visible. Goldsmith (2010, p. 916) notes that scrutiny and denunciation of police officers occur more readily "in the court of public opinion rather than through courts of law and other institutionalized channels of public accountability." We also build upon the focus that this scholarship offers by addressing the court of public opinion as a routinised and mediated process.

The cases covered in this book include entanglements with civilians, private entities like media platforms and public authorities like police. When these agents coalesce, they resemble surveillant assemblages, or temporary partnerships between public and private actors for the purposes of consolidating information about – and attention towards – a target (Haggerty & Ericson, 2000). In response to a case of online harassment, police may work with or solicit information from local social workers, but also digital media users on a global chat forum. With mediated scrutiny and denunciation, one may presume states and police are central agents that initiate and dictate cases of justice-seeking. Surveillant assemblages can indeed serve police investigations, while also enabling other data practices that are "not necessarily established in advance" but instead emerging "from the creative insights of individuals who envision novel possibilities for systems developed for entirely different purposes" (Haggerty, 2006, p. 280). States can temporarily mobilise concerned civilians, prominent figures and media platforms, knowing that these actors may engage in related media practices that are unexpected and not condoned. At a later stage, states can distance themselves from initiatives that they previously supported. This distancing may be explicit, for example condemning the actions of a rogue actor like Russia's *Tesak*, as seen in Chapter 2. But they can also distance themselves implicitly by not taking any steps to maintain or reproduce the temporary bond between state and civilian actors. There is a temporal aspect to state-civilian collaboration. An individual and their vast following can serve as an extension of the omnipresent state for some time and bring social death to other civilians on behalf of the state, until the feeding hand not only halts collaboration but moves to eliminate these civil partners.

Usually this type of state involvement is discussed in relation to countries viewed as more authoritarian, like China and Russia. This is because the state is regarded as more capable of imposing its influence across domains such as educational institutions, mainstream media and even private companies. However, in this chapter we use authoritarianism as an analytical lens instead of a narrowly defined regime. In comparative political science, authoritarianism usually signals regimes with

> limited or restricted pluralism, ideological ambiguity, the over-concentration of power at the executive level—often in the hands of an individual or small clique—, the absence of meaningful checks and balances, low or absent accountability and a rather demobilised or even apathetic (civil) society.
>
> (Katsambekis, 2023, p. 431)

However, due to the trends of populist and illiberal politicians and parties making gains in democratic elections, some researchers propose to study authoritarianism as *practices* that centre around authority and employ actions, policies and discourses that aim to consolidate a strictly ordered society, sabotage accountabilities and counter deviance by means of secrecy, disinformation and disabling voices (ibid.; Glasius, 2018). We adopt the latter perspective to understand state-civilian relations and the court of public opinion.

Participatory authoritarianism and state-civilian relations

Authors writing about Russia and China employ the term 'participatory authoritarianism' to highlight specific aspects of relations between states and civilians under despotic conditions. This concept highlights the role of states in mediated shaming of and by individuals. We add its applications within this media practice specifically, also to speculate whether shaming-based media practices cultivated by states can be found beyond what we typically consider authoritarian countries.

Participatory authoritarianism refers to the semblance of civilians bearing influence on public affairs (including shaming-based outcomes brought to targeted individuals), while at the same time aligning with top-down policies by a ruling political party. It operates within "twin logics of openness and control, pluralism and monism" (Owen, 2020, p. 415), to reconcile global developments, discourses and technological affordances with local regimes, circumstances and cultural practice. In terms of practices, Owen highlights two (ibid., pp. 431–432): limiting access to the 'wrong' kinds of civilian participants such as activists, and engineering participatory events so that they align with a policy decision already made by the state. We can identify specific ways in which these practices may apply to mediated shaming. First, when it comes to state-promoted denunciation of individuals, undesirable participants will encounter technical and organisational obstacles to participation. Second, denunciation by netizens of other individuals may be minimised or misrepresented in public discourse in order to fit a state narrative in terms of who is actually culpable for a given social problem.

Repnikova and Fang (2018) adopt the concept of participatory authoritarianism to address a similar development when looking at the use of new media channels by the Chinese state. They provide a broader understanding of participatory tendencies in authoritarian regimes by noting explicit calls to denounce targets, as well as implicit features of state social media channels to encourage the 'right' kind of netizen participation. Explicit calls include those against celebrities' tax evasion, government officials' corruption as well as unpatriotic behaviour and speech. Implicit features on the other hand include the prominence of anti-feminism content on local platforms, patriotic key opinion leaders (KOLs), police announcements on Sina Weibo as well as the affordance to report illegal or 'harmful' content on social media platforms. This diversity of strategies as well as targets offers an indication of how authoritarian states can mobilise netizens in a routinised manner.

Litvinenko and Toepfl (2019) propose three categories of authoritarian publics at large – leadership-critical, policy-critical and uncritical publics. In the case of Russia, after the 2011–12 mass protests known as *Bolotnaya*, the state took measures to reduce leadership-critical publics and increase the number of uncritical publics (ibid., p. 232). As the state crackdown on dissent in Russia intensified and evolved along with technological advancements, a fourth category of authoritarian publics was proposed by Gabdulhakov (2021) for understanding citizen engagement in politicised content creation: citizen-critical publics. Citizen-critical publics rely on discursive and embodied practices to blame and attack other civilians, accusing them of causing trouble for the country. These acts are in turn broadcast on social and conventional media alike. Citizen-critical publics embody participatory authoritarianism by upholding an illusion of active citizenry in an otherwise oppressive state. In shaping and policing moral boundaries, they typically endorse authoritarian regimes.

As mentioned above, terms like 'authoritarian' are useful for making distinctions between democratic and anti-democratic characteristics in political regimes. But they are also useful for recognising emerging illiberal tendencies and practices in supposed democracies. So while authoritarian countries mobilise their populations in ways that differ from democratic regimes, the term participatory authoritarianism provides a language to describe similar tendencies that we might start to witness on a global scale, emerging either at the political fringes with far-right populist parties, or during states of exception such as pandemics or in response to terrorist acts (Bigo, 2006).

Building on the notion of participatory authoritarianism, we may speculate on the reasons why states encourage civilians to scrutinise and denounce other individuals. One obvious motive is to crowdsource securitisation and surveillance to a volunteer labour pool (cf. Shearing & Wood, 2003). Police forces in many countries encourage civilians to report and submit evidence of suspected cases of child sexual abuse because "the police has limited resources to trace all these individuals, communities and activities hidden in the dark web or private networks." This is according to a Sina Weibo account dedicated to finding and denouncing pedophiles that collects evidence by lurking in relevant chat groups and reporting the perpetrators to the local police. The police praise his behaviour and welcome such denunciations because they lack the resources to oversee a vast digital landscape. In addition to saving law enforcement's resources in fighting crimes by outsourcing certain labour, state appeals can also invoke the notion of a common enemy to strengthen desired ideologies such as patriotism (Huang, 2023). This focus on an 'othered' external target in turn may deflect scrutiny away from a government's own faults and scandals. Finally, mobilising netizens to these ends serves as a channel to receive popular public opinion, allowing moral police to install (in)formal boundaries of actionable conduct. For instance, animal abuse is not yet punishable by law in China, causing public grievances when these cases occur. State-owned media in China such as *People's Daily* do not shy away from reporting and commenting on netizen activities against animal abusers, and sometimes even close their articles by inviting readers to express their opinions about the need for legislation.[13]

We can also consider the motivation for states to suppress civilian scrutiny and denunciation of other individuals. Not only might it serve to re-assert a possible monopolisation of violence as well as appeal to the rule of law, it may also serve to maintain social stability by dampening the emergence of troublesome social movements, as well as discouraging undesirable ideologies such as feminism in China (Wallis, 2015). In several high-profile Chinese #MeToo cases where the accused predators held higher positions in state-affiliated institutions, the accusers and other networked feminist participants immediately faced censorship on platforms and were even arrested without formal prosecution (Yin & Sun, 2021).

The court of public opinion as a reflection of state power

In countries such as China and Russia the state monitors and intervenes in any collective action that might culminate in a social movement (Chen et al., 2016). Equipped with general control over media and other social institutions, authoritarian states can step in at any moment, and their reactions have a signalling effect on the public (Weiss, 2013), who can contribute to how denunciation and shaming cases further develop. In less authoritarian countries, the government can also intervene or take other measures in cases where individuals are denouncing others. Below we propose a working typology of strategies that states may employ to either mitigate or cultivate mediated shaming. These categories distinguish between direct versus indirect forms of intervention, stoking versus suppressing mediated shaming and the use of open versus less visible channels.

Official interventions: partnerships and institutional solutions

States may foster **partnerships with pre-existing civilian groups.** A prominent example of this is when the anti-pedophile group *Perverted Justice* partnered with NBC's *Dateline* to produce the television show *To Catch a Predator*, as they quickly also incorporated local law enforcement into their televised stings of suspected pedophiles. Prior to this coupling, *Perverted Justice* maintained a cooperative relationship with police, and has been praised by various law enforcement agencies in the US (Kohm, 2009). This example combines official support by local state authorities, along with a slick production and recognisable media personality Chris Hansen. Such partnerships legitimate some forms of user-led denunciation, in this case against child sexual abuse. Their explicit message may be that these denunciations are the work of professional partnerships, and that audiences should not engage in pedophile hunting. Yet they also provide a set of protocols for copycats to engage in similar denunciations, typically without state support (Hussey et al., 2022). If states support and participate in circulating content of people denouncing other individuals online, they relinquish control of how audiences will react and interpret to those images of shaming, and cannot assert something resembling a monopolisation of justice and punishment of child sexual abuse. Moreover, we can speculate that states may be aware that further civilian-led punishment of other individuals will be the outcome. As mentioned above, a similar partnership is also enacted to identify and punish pedophiles in China.

States may also **create and fund new civic groups** that have a mandate to watch over others. In these cases, states establish or support the creation of civic groups using digital media to scrutinise and denounce individuals. A prime example of such initiatives could be observed in Russia in the 2010s when various vigilante formations were encouraged and financially supported by the state. These groups came out of a pro-state patriotic youth movement called *Nashi* [Ours]. Some groups such as *StopXam* [Stop a Douchebag][14] specialised in exposing road traffic and parking violations. Activists would confront the perceived offenders and label their vehicles with a sticker reading "I don't care about anyone, I park wherever I want." The confrontations would often escalate into verbal and physical violence. The entire process would be recorded, edited and uploaded on social media by content creators who gained enormous popularity through their YouTube channel and appearances on public television. What made *StopXam* stand out was their fearless confrontation with the 'untouchables' in the country, namely the rich and powerful. In the highly corrupt state, police officers would avoid unnecessary problems and look the other way when they encountered luxurious cars with special licence plates.[15] *StopXam*, on the other hand, would perceive such vehicles as ideal prey, gaining popularity as the people's moral crusaders (Favarel-Garrigues, 2018). Eventually this bold approach to confronting the 'untouchables' backfired against StopXam, as the very state that supported the group's activities demanded its liquidation in court.

While *StopXam* took on the streets, *Hrushi Protiv* [Piggy Against], specialised in exposing 'unscrupulous' merchants for selling expired products. People dressed in pig costumes storm grocery stores in what they call 'raids' and evaluate the products on the shelves. The raids are filmed, edited and uploaded across social media platforms. Store owners and employees may try to stop piggies, once again leading to confrontations and violence, and subsequently more views and reactions by online audiences. *Hrushi Protiv* represents an intricate case in Russia's state-supported denunciation of a marginal community. Over the years, the group voiced an anti-migrant position, claiming that labour migrants from Central Asia and the Caucasus are to blame for expired products in Russia (Gabdulhakov, 2021). Blaming a rightless vulnerable group rather than corporate owners afforded longevity of activism to the group as the 'untouchable' elite expressed no concerns about their work.

States may also **solicit user denunciation in public and privately owned fora**. In these cases, states create or otherwise make use of public and privately owned digital media platforms where civilians can denounce other individuals. In Chapter 2, we saw the example of a viral TikTok user in Venice who was revealed to be a far-right politician at the municipal level. *Cittadini non Distratti* is not only accused of targeting Roma populations as prominent enemies of the state in their public denunciations but specifically uses TikTok and other platforms to do so in a way that appears to align with user-generated input and opinions, whether those users identify as tourists or residents. Due to the assembled nature of media surveillance, many examples include both publicly and privately owned venues that are widely accessible to a national and even global media audience. The Dutch programme *BOOS* [Angry] is broadcast on privately owned YouTube and public broadcaster NPO/BNNVARA.[16] This show serves to publicise grievances that seemingly 'ordinary' individuals bear against other individuals, often in the context of commercial transactions gone awry, but also workplace harassment or discrimination. Denunciation is performed by the show's host Tim Hofman, a journalist working as a public media representative. The show cultivates user comments and responses on its YouTube account with nearly a million subscribers. The descriptions that accompany episodes explicitly ask for public comments that appear below the YouTube video, as well as private emails. In addition, YouTube affords users the ability to post videos in response to official episodes, including light-hearted remixes of tense confrontations. Here a public broadcaster solicits a range of reactions from their audience: watching the episodes, commenting on the grievances they witnessed, submitting ideas of people to denounce to the show's producers and even appearing on the show as the initiator – or target – of a mediated denunciation.

A populist and polarising politician can denounce a private individual on several public and private platforms at once. In these cases the politician may not explicitly call upon their supporters to join in on the attack, but if they have a devoted following such instructions are not necessary, as a crowd-sourced retaliation including digital harassment and threats of physical harm has become commonplace. Consider examples from Donald Trump's presidency in the US. On digital media, Trump has gained a reputation for denouncing and even seeking to cancel countless brands, public figures and private individuals.[17] Denunciation by such a prominent, polarising and media-savvy figure is often guaranteed to mobilise a user-led denunciation and harassment of a target. Not only do supporters feel compelled to harass political targets with vitriol and hate speech, but they may justify such attacks by repeating or building upon a denunciation that a figure like Trump originally broadcasts. After a tense exchange with a college student at a bipartisan event, Trump turned to Twitter to accuse her of being a 'plant' for a rival politician. With no direct appeal to his then nearly five million followers (and countless others who may not be active on Twitter but keep abreast via a broader digital media ecosystem), many of them interpreted this as a call to persecute and harass the eighteen-year-old.[18] Trump – and other public figures who emulate his persona – often have a vacillating relation to the state, at times in power followed by years of influence as an outsider. Yet even when pushed to the margins of state functioning, figures like Trump maintain a seamless ability to mobilise public scrutiny, denunciation and shaming of opponents.

In China, we find specific instances where states direct shaming by the public against the public on the grounds of low-level moral or aesthetic forms of offence, which demonstrate a tendency toward micromanagement in governance (Zhou, 2022). Some local police maintain sections exposing traffic violations on their official websites. Since October 2020, Kaifeng police have published number plates of cars that sped on highways.[19] Elsewhere in Suzhou, local authorities "released pictures of seven people wearing their nightwear" which they denounced as "uncivilised behaviour."[20] In this case, authorities combined photos of the target wearing pyjamas in public, together with their name, identity card and other details. It is important to note that such cases often receive disproportionate attention in Western media like the BBC to depict a dystopian Chinese society under a unified state power, while other developments in China are under-reported. Here the nuanced relationship between central and local government is not provided as context. Further, the portrayal of seemingly dystopian incidents in Western media may serve as inspiration for politicians and populist public figures to propose similar measures in countries like the US and the UK.

States may also **solicit user denunciation via secure channels**. States can appeal to civilians to scrutinise and denounce others through private tip lines and other less visible media. In these examples, the instances of denunciation – and the people being shamed – may not be visible to a broader public, yet the appeal by states for civilians to denounce is publicly visible, as are the mechanisms by which the public should denounce others and possibly one or more high profile cases that exemplify the harm being denounced. We are more likely to find states proposing secure tip lines for civilians to denounce other individuals. These cases occupy a nuanced visibility that combines public and private elements. While social values like privacy, anonymity, dignity and proportionality may be explicitly upheld, the existence and publicity of the tip line itself calls for public attention and scrutiny of certain categories of people, both in private and in public. Prominent examples include the "See something, Say something" campaign in the US[21] as well as the "See it. Say it. Sorted" campaign in the UK.[22] There are instances where a political party may advocate for seemingly confidential denunciations. In the Netherlands, the far-right Forum for Democracy (FvD) called for a tip line to report leftist indoctrination in education.[23] Around the same time, a young student in the Netherlands launched a public Instagram page with the same name and purpose.[24] A marginal political party that holds a few seats in parliament may propose a controversial tip line against a target group, or some other measure to officially stoke resentment against a target population that will provoke public backlash, and not be officially implemented. But due to extensive media coverage, they nevertheless generate exposure of this controversial plan, which may be implemented under more clandestine and bottom-up means. We can distinguish between state-led appeals to denounce via tip lines, and more bottom-up efforts to publish information about targets. Yet it is important to consider the kinds of official and unofficial partnerships and mobilisations that occur within a shared political climate and media environment.

In less obvious cases, local authorities may direct public scrutiny to a criminal suspect, and not explicitly call for their denunciation and shaming. Yet given the status of the crime, there may be a reasonable expectation that such an appeal for information is accompanied by public revulsion and denunciation. In 2006, Canadian police turned to the internet to help identify a person who urinated on a war memorial statue in Ottawa. Photos of the suspect were shared via public and privately owned media.[25] No explicit denunciation was solicited by the state, but given the nature of the offence, we can still expect a visible expression of disgust in comments and editorials. This appeal by the police may seem innocuous, and some might even accuse the police of negligence if they chose not to take advantage of public knowledge of this type of incident. Yet these appeals to the public often work via social media platforms that generate vitriolic comments from the public by design, especially when the incident is perceived to be morally inexcusable. These appeals also take place via tabloids that supplemented police statements with their own vitriol,[26] alongside comments sourced from the public.[27] We can expect the state to operate with a reasonable understanding of its population's cultural mores, and perhaps also a reasonable understanding of a broader media audience that includes people with limited to no connection to their country. In choosing to make public appeals about high-profile, controversial and provocative crimes, states may knowingly mobilise a mediated backlash against the target, including harassment and threats of physical harm.

Unofficial interventions: signaling support and co-opting concerned individuals

In addition to the official support and solicitation of participation, the state can also adopt more **subtle means to intervene in mediated shaming incidents**. To find these unofficial interventions that imply state attitudes towards local concerns, we identify traces in media and public spheres, including in countries where the government has a tighter grip over media. We do not maintain a rigid distinction between official and unofficial signals of support, especially in media environments where unofficial channels like social media accounts are de facto extensions of political communication. In China, it is common practice for the government to provide discursive support for certain individuals, actions and collective sentiments via media outlets, especially those run by the state. When civilian denunciations align with the state's agenda or ideologies, such as the promotion of nationalism, state-run media such as *People's Daily* publish articles that concur in and amplify the participants' discourse and join the public shaming towards the target. In four high-profile cases where Chinese female intellectuals were targeted for their "unpatriotic speech," state-run media followed netizens in shaming the targets as ungrateful traitors (Huang, 2023). In doing so the party-state has developed strategies to co-opt populist and nationalist sentiments to maintain domestic cohesion and stability as well as the CPC's ruling position (Repnikova & Fang, 2018). Such signalling effects (Pan et al., 2022) have been accepted as common knowledge and usually expected by Chinese citizens. In many cases, the participants will comment "let's wait and see what *yangmei* [央媒, state media] say."

As seen above in the case of *Nashi*, financial support from states may happen officially, when they allocate public funds to civil groups that scrutinise and denounce the 'right' kinds of social harms. But states can also ensure financial support to these groups indirectly, by directing public attention to groups via positive media exposure, with this public then poised to donate to their cause or provide other kinds of material support or capital. In the US, the Twitter account *LibsofTikTok* has become a prominent forum to openly denounce ideological opponents of the American right. The previously anonymous administrator of the account relies on submissions from followers, and garners extensive prominence from supporters and opponents. In addition to gaining support from right-wing media figures, Republican political actors like Florida's press secretary signalled their support for the account.[28] A Republican State Senator appointed *LibsofTikTok*'s administrator to Oklahoma's Library Media Advisory Committee, a move that sparked protest from a polarised electorate.[29]

Negative approaches: denouncing and suppressing denunciation

Beyond the many ways states can stoke and seek to benefit from user-led denunciation, they may also suppress at least some instances of such scrutiny, effectively dampening more troublesome forms of civilian input. States may **formally punish participants** after mediated shaming is initiated by the public. Local authorities can choose to legally sanction individuals and groups that publicly shame others, especially if there is a clear violation of laws in the process, as when the public confrontation of suspected pedophiles results in forcible confinement.[30] In the case of child sexual exploitation police are in a difficult position, as they may not want to formally support groups that make public accusations of child sexual abuse against targets. Yet at the same time they may not want to appear to be ineffective in targeting a high-profile crime that mobilises large-scale public denunciation. Even though "the investigatory practices of paedophile hunters are antithetical to numerous core values and functions of the criminal justice system," scholars note that the sensitive nature of the offence means that "[pedophile] hunters are seldom prosecuted for falsely imprisoning their targets" (Purshouse, 2020, pp. 385, 394).

Some clandestine online communities publish content about local concerns in a way that exploits the dignity of marginalised groups. In Canada, the *Thunder Bay Dirty* Facebook page provoked a police response, notably as the page largely contained photographs and derogatory messages about First Nations people.[31] The mayor and other residents denounced the page on the grounds of discrimination against a vulnerable population. Both the creator of the page as well as an administrator of a separate page calling for its removal note that they received threats on social media, and for this reason, both express a hesitancy to speak openly with the press about their respective involvement in this case.

Official punishment or suppression of denunciation is usually case-specific. Most states have not formed consistent legal or administrative principles in dealing with the (potential) harms brought by this phenomenon. States usually adopt a negative approach to these incidents when there are disproportionately severe consequences (e.g. targets committing suicide due to unbearable harassment, such as "the pink hair girl incident"[32]) or potential threats to state power (mostly in authoritarian countries, such as some Chinese #MeToo incidents mentioned earlier). However, due to the participatory nature of mediated denunciation and difficulties in pinpointing responsible individuals, it is more common to see the suppression of the mobilisation instead of legal prosecution of individuals.

State authorities may also take **other measures against** user-led denunciation. In addition to the Dutch anti-doxing laws described at the start of this chapter, the Canadian privacy watchdog requested that a telecom company in the Northwest Territories take down Facebook posts in which they identified customers who had not paid their bills.[33] The company not only published the names and debt amounts on their own Facebook page, but also shared the list with several local community pages on the platform. There other users could comment and join in on the denunciation, but also launch a counter-denunciation against the telecom worker who took these steps, and who was also identified by their full name. As online shaming and harassment in general become common practices and tactics in China, the party-state grew concerned about the broader consequences. In accordance with the party-state's effort to regulate and prevent *wangbao* [网暴/网络暴力, online violence], several state media outlets in China also published opinion pieces to criticise this phenomenon. In June 2023, Xinhua News Agency stated that "platforms are the frontline of stopping online violence [...] the platforms' responsibility is more than just banning several accounts; they should put social order and people's security before boosting traffic [on platforms] for their own profits."[34]

Broader institutional strategies

Other **legal and infrastructural strategies** can bring a positive or negative impact on civilian-led denunciations. These types of developments may be generalised and unintentional in cases where they are not explicitly in response to a specific case of user-led denunciation. This builds on an earlier appeal to understand how mediated shaming may be "shaped by factors including legislation, social media platform terms of use, journalistic practices and standards" (Trottier, 2020, p. 204), notably as a method for states to cultivate more acceptable forms of civilian input. In terms of state-led strategies in relation to the press landscape, Dutch media provide protection to criminal suspects by identifying them with initials instead of their full name. They also avoid disclosing suspects' ethnicity. These steps are meant to protect a suspect's family and community to which they belong, including against retaliatory scrutiny, denunciation, shaming and violence (Fullerton & Patterson, 2021). As it happens, a Dutch anti-racism agency has advocated for publishing the ethnicity of suspects, as in some cases the current protective measures have seemed to exacerbate polarisation and scrutiny within concerned neighbourhoods.[35] We can also identify state-led strategies in relation to the digital media landscape and technological affordances more broadly. The Chinese state and digital platforms have developed various technological mechanisms to hold users accountable for their online speech and conduct, such as the *wangluo shiming zhi* [网络实名制, internet real-name system] that requires individual users to register their real ID and phone number when using digital services since 2012,[36] the *jubao* [举报, reporting] features embedded in almost every social media platform (Ye et al., 2024) since 2016, as well as public displaying provincial and foreign country location details of all users' IP addresses since 2022.[37]

In terms of state-led strategies in relation to judicial processes, the US *Speak Out Act* was implemented in response to #MeToo in order to restrict enforcement of non-disclosure agreements in cases of sexual assault and harassment at the workplace (Bullock & Hersch, 2024). New laws also criminalise civilian activity and signal to its population that these new crimes should be denounced. After the invasion of Ukraine in 2022, a series of laws were adopted in Russia making it a crime to discredit the armed forces, or even refer to the invasion as 'war.' The new politics of fear established a system of total control over public discourse, forcing any disagreeing voice to leave the country and silencing those who could not escape. In the southern city of Krasnodar, a couple was arrested in a restaurant when other diners overheard their critical conversation and called the police.[38] Lenin's dream outlined in Chapter 2 became true, as citizens in Russia engage in wholesale denunciation. Yet it also remains clear that the role of the police in Russia did not wither away. In fact, there is a state-citizen syndicate that is mediated by police. When denouncing other civilians for opposing the state, these concerned individuals rely on the police as the ultimate punisher.

Leaving online shitstorms alone

Anybody observing incivility on digital media may ask why states neglect to shut down online shaming. We can reflect on how to describe and conceptualise a state approach to shaming that may resemble an absence of a response. Leaving mediated shaming alone means that a state has (temporarily) chosen to overlook persecution seemingly taking place under its jurisdiction. There are diverse reasons why this may be the case. State actors may believe the incident is too minor to garner an official response, and thus greater public attention (cf. Broll & Huey, 2015). Surely not all instances of civilians airing grievances about other civilians will warrant a response from a state's limited capacities. A state may be unsure of an appropriate strategy, especially in cases of novel forms of denunciation, novel offences being denounced or in cases where grievances reflect ideological struggles which states may prefer to avoid. A governing party may risk alienating part of their electorate by taking a stand for or against mediated shaming of parking violations in an urban centre marked by a cultural divide between cyclists and drivers. State inactivity may be due to a perception by local authorities that the form of shaming is proportionate to the harm being denounced. In other cases, the scale of the denunciation may be acknowledged to be excessive, but still acceptable if the target engaged in offences that are recognised as long-neglected problems, for instance in denunciations against racism and sexual assault in a post-#BLM and post-#MeToo context. Finally, state authorities may simply allege to be unaware of a given shaming incident.

Some may interpret state inactivity as condoning the user-led shaming in question, while others may interpret this inaction differently. A polarised audience with diverging interpretations of mediated shaming incidents and public reactions will likely also have opposing interpretations of state inaction (Ahlstrand, 2021). This may in turn reinforce their respective commitment to mediated shaming as an alternative to conventional justice-seeking, based on a perceived unwillingness or inability by the state to do so. When a state chooses to intervene in one instance of user-led shaming and not intervene in another, it signals to its population what types of shaming are permitted.

And these signals may be interpreted differently by segments of a polarised civil population, thus exacerbating perceptions that communities cannot rely on state authorities for (social) justice, and must rely on their own (digital) means of scrutiny, denunciation and shaming (cf. Johnston, 1996). Regardless of what a country's government thinks of any political faction and the backlash it generates, progressive and conservative communities may both believe that the state is choosing to ignore public denunciations and related harms against them (cf. Gebrihet & Mwale, 2024).

Conclusion

When reflecting on global patterns in participatory authoritarianism, two takeaways are apparent. First, we claim that digital statecraft in Russia and China can serve as a potential global model of participatory authoritarianism. Russia upholds vigilante statecraft (cf. Favarel-Garrigues & Gayer,2024) by mobilising its population to denounce what it considers threats to alleged national interests, a phenomenon that we also witness in China as well as among more authoritarian figures elsewhere. Under these conditions, the court of public opinion is configured to systematically exclude vulnerable 'enemies of the state' from participating, while placing them in the crosshairs of crowdsourced denunciation and material harm. As Sina Weibo developed and became one of the most popular social media platforms in China, more government branches set up official accounts. Police agencies at provincial, county, municipal and district levels formally and informally encourage citizens to report on illegal conduct. Less authoritarian states may cultivate similar partnerships with netizens and local media platforms, whether they wish to cope with limited resources, assert a common enemy or gauge popular sentiment on emerging harms.

Second, we acknowledge the temporality in modes of state involvement and support of mediated shaming, as states can easily shift from support to censorship of mobilised digital media users. In the 2010s, the Russian state kept digitally savvy and socially active youth on a short leash by supporting them financially and otherwise endorsing them (Gabdulhakov, 2019). As authoritarian inclinations of the state progressed, vigilantes were 'audited' and those who posed a threat to the regime in one way or another were hobbled or eliminated, while those who supported the political status quo continued operation. Scholarship on participatory authoritarianism provides valuable insights into the ways governing bodies strategically mobilise certain forms of 'citizen' participation to largely deny a wider range of civil liberties. We aim to underline the mercurial nature of these partnerships, as states may move from condoning to condemning so-called concerned individuals participating in courts of public opinion. This volatility is not only due to authoritarian pursuits of states consolidating and maintaining power, but also due to the volatility of digital media platforms that may amplify the visibility and social impact of mediated shaming, beyond local national borders to reach an unanticipated global audience. Observing the relation between a state and media at one point in time provides little indication of how either the state or platform operators may upend their partnership. We also must account for democratic and less-democratic transfers of power, where one political party may do away with the policies and programmes of rival predecessors.

We can also question whether the temporary nature of state support – in whatever form it takes – always reflects a deliberate state strategy, or if other factors are at play. In other words, do states always decide when they relinquish support of a civilian-led justice-seeking group, and do they always benefit from these decisions? Finally, civilians can also change the nature of their cooperation with states. The court of public opinion – understood as civilians using platforms – is also perpetually in a liminal position between a tool for the state, and something beyond state control. Partnerships between states and civilians in denouncing other civilians are generally presumed to be fleeting. Looking forward, we identify the mobilisation of outrage among populist political groups as a development for readers to follow. In seemingly non-authoritarian countries, regressive populist parties may engage in digital media practices that help advance authoritarian characteristics – including restrictions on public expression – by mobilising supporters who in turn scrutinise and denounce targeted communities for moral, cultural and legal offences.

Notes

1 https://nltimes.nl/2021/07/12/netherlands-make-doxing-criminal-offense
2 https://www.at5.nl/artikelen/204982/halsema-wil-handhaving-verder-aanscherpen-feestje-in-de-buurt-laat-het-weten
3 https://www.rtlnieuws.nl/nieuws/politiek/artikel/4656656/woede-om-meldpunt-forum-over-indoctrinatie-onderwijs
4 http://www.news.cn/legal/2023-07/07/c_1129737397.htm; http://www.moj.gov.cn/pub/sfbgw/lfyjzj/lflfyjzj/202307/t20230707_482196.html; http://www.cac.gov.cn/2022-11/04/c_1669204414682178.htm
5 https://www.hrw.org/news/2024/02/15/russia-first-convictions-under-lgbt-extremist-ruling
6 https://zona.media/news/2024/01/31/serezhki
7 As stated earlier in this book, we acknowledge that the term citizen excludes those who do not hold citizenship, yet are still at the mercy of both a state's local authorities and mobilised populace. While there may be a stated focus on citizens and citizenship in state appeals, it is important to include a wider civilian population who may not only be targeted by such appeals, but may also identify with a given citizenry and participate in the denunciations described in this chapter.
8 https://sports.yahoo.com/blogs/nhl-puck-daddy/vancouver-police-increase-heat-riot-suspects-wanted-poster-154002731.html , see also Schneider and Trottier (2012).
9 https://macleans.ca/news/canada/the-toronto-police-let-the-jays-beer-thrower-and-all-of-us-down/

10 https://weibo.com/ttarticle/p/show?id=2309404974443004035097
11 See the Canadian public broadcaster's reactions to the Toronto Police's solicitation of public information on digital media: https://www.cbc.ca/news/canada/toronto/beer-can-throw-blue-jays-baltimore-orioles-1.3794214
12 https://nos.nl/artikel/341031-polenmeldpunt-wie-klaagt-over-wie
13 See for example articles entitled "The animal abusers only get moral judgement; do we need special legislation?": https://wap.peopleapp.com/article/6056501/5969299
14 The literal translation is 'stop a road boor,' but the group itself uses 'stop a douche-bag' on its social media.
15 Licence plate numbers are coded in Russia. A vehicle with a Moscow city licence plate containing zeros or 'pretty' numbers such as 777 is a sign of wealth and connections with powerful people. Police officers prefer to avoid conflict with these car owners.
16 https://npo.nl/npo3/boos/over
17 https://www.mercurynews.com/2020/07/07/trump-rails-against-cancel-culture-but-embraced-it-in-the-past/
18 https://www.washingtonpost.com/politics/this-is-what-happens-when-donald-trump-attacks-a-private-citizen-on-twitter/2016/12/08/a1380ece-bd62-11e6-91ee-1adddfe36cbe_story.html
19 http://gaj.kaifeng.gov.cn/jsp/goto?p=search&siteId=1&key_word=%E6%9B%9D%E5%85%89%E5%8F%B0&page=1&rows=10&pages=5
20 https://www.bbc.com/news/world-asia-china-51188669
21 https://www.dhs.gov/see-something-say-something; see also Reeves (2012)
22 https://www.btp.police.uk/police-forces/british-transport-police/areas/campaigns/see-it-say-it-sorted/
23 https://www.rtlnieuws.nl/nieuws/politiek/artikel/4656656/woede-om-meldpunt-forum-over-indoctrinatie-onderwijs; https://www.ewmagazine.nl/nederland/achtergrond/2019/03/4-vragen-over-fvd-meldpunt-voor-docenten-680496/
24 https://www.rtlnieuws.nl/editienl/artikel/4626271/mats-verzet-zich-op-instagram-tegen-linkse-indoctrinatie-onderwijs; https://revu.nl/artikel/1674/de-nieuwe-posterboy-van-alt-right-is-maar-een-jankerd
25 https://www.cbc.ca/news/canada/ottawa/police-seeking-revellers-who-urinated-on-ottawa-memorial-1.573199
26 (July 5, 2006). War memorial miscreants need remedial education. *The Vancouver Sun* (British Columbia). https://advance.lexis.com/api/document?collection=news&id=urn:contentItem:4KBD-2GJ0-TWD4-0371-00000-00&context=1516831
27 Mike Harvey. (July 5, 2006). Disgusting and thoughtless act a display of ignorance. *The Vancouver Sun* (British Columbia). https://advance.lexis.com/api/document?collection=news&id=urn:contentItem:4KBD-2GJ0-TWD4-0372-00000-00&context=1516831.
28 https://www.washingtonpost.com/technology/2022/04/19/libs-of-tiktok-right-wing-media/
29 https://midmichigannow.com/news/nation-world/libs-of-tiktok-creators-appointment-to-oklahoma-library-committee-sparks-protest-chaya-raichik-right-wing-creator-social-media-influence-state-library-books
30 https://www.theguardian.com/world/2023/mar/31/canada-arrest-pedophile-hunting-group-explicit-images
31 https://www.huffpost.com/archive/ca/entry/thunder-bay-dirty-facebook-page-sparks-police-investigation-a_n_7154476
32 https://www.scmp.com/news/people-culture/trending-china/article/3210853/bullied-death-millions-chinese-mourn-after-prostitute-pink-hair-taunts-drive-woman-23-suicide

33 https://www.cbc.ca/news/canada/north/privacy-commissioner-senga-services-1.3347760
34 http://www.news.cn/mrdx/2023-06/29/c_1310730068.htm
35 https://www.expatica.com/nl/general/call-to-disclose-crime-suspects-ethnicity-38891/
36 https://web.archive.org/web/20130203205216/http://www.npc.gov.cn/npc/xinwen/2012-12/29/content_1749526.htm
37 https://www.businessinsider.com/china-social-platforms-to-make-user-locations-visible-ip-addresses-2022-4?international=true&r=US&IR=T
38 https://theins.ru/en/news/258994

References

Ahlstrand, J. L. (2021). Strategies of ideological polarisation in the online news media: A social actor analysis of Megawati Soekarnoputri. *Discourse & Society*, *32*(1), 64–80. https://doi.org/10.1177/0957926520961634

Amann, P. H. (1983). Vigilante fascism: The black legion as an American hybrid. *Comparative Studies in Society and History*, *25*(3), 490–524. https://doi.org/10.1017/s0010417500010550

Barney, D., Coleman, G., Ross, C., Sterne, J., & Tembeck, T. (Eds.). (2016). *The participatory condition in the digital age*. University of Minnesota Press.

Bigo, D. (2006). Security, exception, ban and surveillance. In D. Lyon (Ed.), *Theorizing surveillance: The panopticon and beyond* (pp. 46–68). Routledge. https://doi.org/10.4324/9781843926818-5

Broll, R., & Huey, L. (2015). "Just being mean to somebody isn't a police matter": Police perspectives on policing cyberbullying. *Journal of School Violence*, *14*(2), 155–176. https://doi.org/10.1080/15388220.2013.879367

Bullock, B. D., & Hersch, J. (2024). The impact of banning confidential settlements on discrimination dispute resolution. *Vanderbilt Law Review*, *77*, 23–39. https://doi.org/10.2139/ssrn.4562380

Chen, J., Pan, J., & Xu, Y. (2016). Sources of authoritarian responsiveness: A field experiment in China. *American Journal of Political Science*, *60*(2), 383–400. https://doi.org/10.1111/ajps.12207

Favarel-Garrigues, G. (2018). Vigilantism and moral crusades in contemporary Russia. *Revue Française de Science Politique*, *68*(4), 651–667. https://doi.org/10.3917/rfsp.684.0651

Favarel-Garrigues, G., & Gayer, L. (2024). *Proud to punish: The global landscapes of rough justice*. Stanford University Press. https://doi.org/10.1515/9781503637689

Fullerton, R. S., & Patterson, M. J. (2021). *Murder in our midst: Comparing crime coverage ethics in an age of globalized news*. Oxford University Press. https://doi.org/10.1093/oso/9780190863531.001.0001

Gabdulhakov, R. (2019). Heroes or hooligans? Media portrayal of StopXam (Stop a Douchebag) vigilantes in Russia. *Laboratorium. Журнал социальных исследований*, *11*(3), 16–45. https://doi.org/10.25285/2078-1938-2019-11-3-16-45

Gabdulhakov, R. (2021). Media control and citizen-critical publics in Russia: Are some "pigs" more equal than others? *Media and Communication*, *9*(4), 62–72. https://doi.org/10.17645/mac.v9i4.4233

Galtung, J. (1990). Cultural violence. *Journal of Peace Research*, *27*(3), 291–305. https://doi.org/10.1177/0022343390027003005

Gebrihet, H. G., & Mwale, M. L. (2024). The effects of polarisation on trust in government: Evidence from Ethiopia. *Transforming Government: People, Process and Policy*. https://doi.org/10.1108/TG-09-2023-0130

Glasius, M. (2018). What authoritarianism is… and is not: A practice perspective. *International Affairs*, *94*(3), 515–533. https://doi.org/10.1093/ia/iiy060

Goff, W. (2011). The shades of grey of cyberbullying in Australian schools. *Australian Journal of Education*, *55*(2), 176–181. https://doi.org/10.1177/000494411105500207

Goldsmith, A. J. (2010). Policing's new visibility. *The British Journal of Criminology*, *50*(5), 914–934. https://doi.org/10.1093/bjc/azq033.

Haggerty, K. D. (2006). Tear down the walls: On demolishing the panopticon. In D. Lyon (Ed.), *Theorizing surveillance: The panopticon and beyond* (pp. 37–59). Routledge. https://doi.org/10.4324/9781843926818-4

Haggerty, K. D., & Ericson, R. V. (2000). The surveillant assemblage. *British Journal of Sociology*, *51*(4), 605–622. https://doi.org/10.1080/00071310020015280

Huang, Q. (2023). The discursive construction of populist and misogynist nationalism: Digital vigilantism against unpatriotic intellectual women in China. *Social Media + Society*, *9*(2). https://doi.org/10.1177/20563051231170816

Hussey, E., Richards, K., & Scott, J. (2022). Pedophile hunters and performing masculinities online. *Deviant Behavior*, *43*(11), 1313–1330. https://doi.org/10.1080/01639625.2021.1978278

Johnston, L. (1996). What is vigilantism?. *The British Journal of Criminology*, *36*(2), 220–236. https://doi.org/10.1093/oxfordjournals.bjc.a014083

Katsambekis, G. (2023). Mainstreaming authoritarianism. *The Political Quarterly*, *94*(3), 428–436. https://doi.org/10.1111/1467-923x.13299

Kohm, S. A. (2009). Naming, shaming and criminal justice: Mass-mediated humiliation as entertainment and punishment. *Crime, Media, Culture*,*5*(2), 188–205. https://doi.org/10.1177/1741659009335724

Lippert, R., & Wilkinson, B. (2010). Capturing crime, criminals and the public's imagination: Assembling crime stoppers and CCTV surveillance. *Crime, Media, Culture*, *6*(2), 131–152. https://doi.org/10.1177/1741659010369950

Litvinenko, A., & Toepfl, F. (2019). The "gardening" of an authoritarian public at large: How Russia's ruling elites transformed the country's media landscape after the 2011/12 protests "for fair elections." *Publizistik*, *64*(2), 225–240. https://doi.org/10.1007/s11616-019-00486-2

Liu, Z., Lin, S., Lu, T., Shen, Y., & Liang, S. (2023). Towards a constructed order of co-governance: Understanding the state–society dynamics of neighbourhood collaborative responses to COVID-19 in urban China. *Urban Studies*, *60*(9), 1730–1749. https://doi.org/10.1177/00420980221081314

Lub, V. (2018). Neighbourhood watch: Mechanisms and moral implications. *The British Journal of Criminology*, *58*(4), 906–924. https://doi.org/10.1093/bjc/azx058

Lyon, D. (2001). *Surveillance society: Monitoring everyday life*. Open University Press.

Miliband, R. (1969). *The state in capitalist society*. New York: Basic Books.

Owen, C. (2020). Participatory authoritarianism: From bureaucratic transformation to civic participation in Russia and China. *Review of International Studies*, *46*(4), 415–434. https://doi.org/10.1017/S0260210520000248

Pan, J., Shao, Z., & Xu, Y. (2022). How government-controlled media shifts policy attitudes through framing. *Political Science Research and Methods, 10*(2), 317–332. https://doi.org/10.1017/psrm.2021.35

Purshouse, J. (2020). 'Paedophile hunters', criminal procedure, and fundamental human rights. *Journal of Law and Society, 47*(3), 384–411. https://doi.org/10.1111/jols.12235

Reeves, J. (2012). If you see something, say something: Lateral surveillance and the uses of responsibility. *Surveillance & Society, 10*(3/4), 235–248. https://doi.org/10.24908/ss.v10i3/4.4209

Repnikova, M., & Fang, K. (2018). Authoritarian participatory persuasion 2.0: Netizens as thought work collaborators in China. *Journal of Contemporary China, 27*(113), 763–779. https://doi.org/10.1080/10670564.2018.1458063

Schneider, C. J., & Trottier, D. (2012). The 2011 Vancouver riot and the role of Facebook in crowd-sourced policing. *BC Studies: The British Columbian Quarterly*, (175), 57–72. https://doi.org/10.14288/bcs.v0i175.182403

Shearing, C., & Wood, J. (2003). Nodal governance, democracy, and the new 'denizens'. *Journal of Law and Society, 30*(3), 400–419. https://doi.org/10.1111/1467-6478.00263

Tomba, L. (2014). *The government next door: Neighborhood politics in Urban China.* Cornell University Press. https://doi.org/10.7591/9780801455209

Trottier, D. (2020). Denunciation and doxing: Towards a conceptual model of digital vigilantism. *Global Crime, 21*(3–4), 196–212. https://doi.org/10.1080/17440572.2019.1591952

Trottier, D., & Fuchs, C. (2014). Theorising social media, politics and the state: An introduction. In D. Trottier & C. Fuchs (Eds.), *Social media, politics and the state* (pp. 3–38). Routledge. https://doi.org/10.4324/9781315764832

Wallis, C. (2015). Gender and China's online censorship protest culture. *Feminist Media Studies, 15*(2), 223–238. https://doi.org/10.1080/14680777.2014.928645

Weiss, J. C. (2013). Authoritarian signaling, mass audiences, and nationalist protest in China. *International Organization, 67*(1), 1–35. http://doi.org/10.1017/S0020818312000380

Ye, Z., Huang, Q., & Krijnen, T. (2024). Douyin's playful platform governance: Platform's self-regulation and content creators' participatory surveillance. *International Journal of Cultural Studies.*https://doi.org/10.1177/13678779241247065

Yin, S., & Sun, Y. (2021). Intersectional digital feminism: Assessing the participation politics and impact of the MeToo movement in China. *Feminist Media Studies, 21*(7), 1176–1192. http://doi.org/10.1080/14680777.2020.1837908

Young, S. (2020). More eyes on crime?: The rhetoric of mediated mugshots. In D. Trottier, R. Gabdulhakov, & Q. Huang (Eds.),*Introducing vigilant audiences* (pp. 307–330). Open Book Publishers. https://doi.org/10.11647/obp.0200.12

Zhou, X. (2022). *The logic of governance in China: An organizational approach.* Cambridge University Press. https://doi.org/10.1017/9781009159418

6 Conclusion

From the court of public opinion to the reputational stock market

In 2021 a new type of social media platform emerged that allowed users to buy and sell cryptocurrency linked to other users' public standing. People could effectively invest and divest in the reputations of others. The platform describes how this valuation could fluctuate: "if Elon Musk succeeds in landing the first person on Mars, his coin price should theoretically go up. And if, in contrast, he makes a racial slur during a press conference, his coin price should theoretically go down."[1] BitClout's launch generated controversy, in part because prominent individuals in and beyond Silicon Valley discovered that their image and profile were already present on the platform without their consent.[2] Critics have also noted that such a platform incentivises people "to cancel people" as one can gain financially by "open[ing] a short position and then try[ing] to angle someone's reputation."[3] Though we have covered reputational harm extensively in previous chapters, BitClout points to underexplored ways to harm others' public standing through disproportionate and unwarranted punishment. Targets of denunciation already suffer material consequences through job loss and review bombing. BitClout expands on this potential for abuse by mapping personal reputation onto financial crimes.

Public pushback against BitClout is only the latest attempt to test and scope out new ethics and protocols for the appropriate handling of other people's reputations in a heavily mediated world. Denunciation and social sanction are ramped up through domestically available technologies, media cultures based on pervasive disputes and grievances, as well as a political and economic climate marked by polarisation and precarity. Following the last four chapters, we may ask who governs the court of public opinion: concerned individuals, influencers and other prominent users, media platforms or states? Ultimately no single group has sole exclusive control over denunciation and shaming processes. Yet a common theme in our interviews and other data is how platforms and states shape the ways in which people watch over others. In many ways, we see a return to a familiar paradox with pre-digital vigilantism: individual users are empowered with the ability to name, shame and

DOI: 10.4324/9781003453017-6

punish targeted individuals, yet these actions often reflect hegemonic values such as ethno-racial supremacy and law and order politics (Abrahams, 1998). Moreover, they may be encouraged and compelled, but also sanctioned and suppressed by states. As we see, content creators alongside other media actors like moderators and (temporarily) prominent individuals also command tremendous influence in stoking, amplifying and rebuking vigilant individuals.

Not only are new morals and offences shaped through media practice (such as raising awareness of microaggressions or antisocial behaviour), but the very practice of calling out these harms is itself widely contested. And while some people may oppose excessive denunciations as a whole, we are more likely to encounter a selective denunciation of denunciations, that in turn justifies an ideological curation of grievances. Conservative media figures may claim to reject cancel culture when speaking of the left's public engagements, but those same individuals also denounce and cast visibility upon their opponents – often the same people they accuse of zealotry – with the intent of bringing material harm to their careers. Mediated visibility thus remains a contested terrain. Contestation of appropriate forms of social visibility is not new (cf. Thompson, 2005), yet contemporary digital media extend these concerns to a range of public figures like entrepreneurs, influencers and content creators. They are also extended to certain kinds of precarious labourers who need to augment their own visibility to make an appeal to a public when searching for employment (Vallas & Christin, 2018), or engaging in crowdfunding (Wade, 2022). In the coming years, we expect a growing routinisation of scrutiny and denunciation of individuals through social platforms, including crowdfunding and reviewing sites. These sites make up a digital media landscape that facilitates status degradation ceremonies as media rituals (Garfinkel, 1956; cf. Couldry, 2002).

More generally, we can reflect on what is meant by appearing in public. Does it involve a ubiquitous risk of exposure and reputational harm? Such a claim verges on paranoia. Yet this paranoia seems to be vindicated when paying attention to the daily procession of shameful revelations in tabloids on social media news feeds, instead of all the moments where people's immoral, problematic or otherwise discrediting personal details remain out of public view. Being public-facing means being held accountable to social norms that, for example, prohibit gendered and racialised abuse in popular media, or in the private lives of entertainers and other public figures. Yet due to cultural and political polarisation, taking a stand against racial and gendered abuse – or simply belonging to a vulnerable or marginal community – can also be grounds for enhanced mediated scrutiny and denunciation. We also witness cultural pushback against excessive interpersonal social scrutiny, in which people watch over others and report on offences through a mediated public. For instance, people may recognise and be antagonised by the sight of someone pointing a camera at them in public. Popular culture also seems to reflect a disapproval of excessive forms of scrutiny in public-facing settings. Surveillant imaginaries of appropriate and inappropriate scrutiny and shaming are still in formation and are shaped by high-profile incidents, popular culture and the efforts of popular commentators and opinion leaders.

Reflecting on mediated denunciation

The court of public opinion is often recognised as an online shitstorm. To determine why this is the case, the previous four chapters provide insights about global media conditions. These takeaways potentially apply across cultural and institutional contexts. In Chapter 2, when focusing on concerned individuals, we see that local contexts – whether regional or professional – are grounds for scrutiny and shaming. Mediated shaming is both a global practice and one where people are compelled by their immediate surroundings. These surroundings can also be a point of vulnerability and possible harm, as seen with those under watch by *GeenStijl*, and more severely in the plight of Kyrgyz migrant women accused of betraying their home country. And women are clearly subject to persistent and disproportionate forms of scrutiny and shaming through local and global networks (cf. Gill, 2023), along with other marginalised communities. It is therefore not a matter of a trade-off between the global virality of an incident, and its local relevance and virulence. Local grievances easily become viral pile-ons, and when denunciations spread they continue to bring harm to local and vulnerable communities.

When focusing on prominent individuals in Chapter 3, mediated visibility is both a prerequisite for any degree of success and a means to a downfall. Visibility is both a trap and a paycheque. This means conditions of visibility more generally are not solely negative, a fact that those studying surveillance practices need to acknowledge. Savvy media actors like influencers and content creators – much like conventional celebrities and their publicity teams – quickly develop a sense of beneficial and harmful forms of exposure. Yet visibility deemed to be beneficial in one context may lead to denunciation when taken out of that context. A Twitter thread may bring viral recognition and eventually lead to social sanction from a wider public.[4] Moreover, accumulating positive public recognition may also bring a kind of "antifan" scrutiny (cf. Gray, 2005) where people seek discrediting details about someone, simply because of their rise to prominence. Consider the practice of vigilant audiences digging up problematic tweets belonging to someone who suddenly attains online fame. Chapter 3 also highlights how cancel culture discourse simultaneously marks both a contestation and a normalisation of denunciation, and specifically a normalisation of reputational shitstorms transcending regional boundaries. Being 'against cancel culture,' therefore, is by itself not effective for combating excessive and abusive forms of scrutiny and shaming.

At the very least, this requires a critical self-reflection on one's own position when it comes to highly disputed and polarising cases of social sanction.

In Chapter 4, when focusing on platforms, the so-called engagement economy is in a vampiric relation with people's reputations. Social media platforms derive capital by cultivating social engagement by targeting the reputation of those found on these sites, reputation itself understood as an occasionally tangible form of capital. Platform operators serve a steady stream of content to users, by bringing harm to those same kinds of people. A common theme that persists in the cases explored in this book is that justice and accountability – and even mild rebukes – should have instead taken place elsewhere. Digital media platforms are a suboptimal location for social sanction. The possibility that people do not intervene directly in embodied settings – like confronting someone being antisocial on a train – is both a common criticism of so-called "keyboard warriors,"[5] as well as a justification for mediated shaming.

In Chapter 5, states regard online mobs and the court of public opinion as something that they may see themselves as needing to manage and exploit. There is a diverse range of strategies they may adopt, many of which indirectly prime a mediated audience to watch over and denounce a target or targeted population. Scholars writing about participatory authoritarianism capture some of these steps, yet in our typology, we also see a much broader range of moves states can make to either quell or mobilise online civic outrage. And while we often frame countries like China and Russia as authoritarian to distinguish them from Western democracies, our typology suggests that democracies already stoke and otherwise intervene in online shitstorms.

Across chapters we also see that various types of actors converge on digital media to handle interpersonal grievances. Acknowledging this fact calls attention to three points of tension when conceiving of online shitstorms. First, we identify a tension between a general perception that nobody is responsible for online shitstorms, and that a particular actor or set of actors is responsible. This is a struggle for both scholarly understandings of denunciations, but also how they are understood in the media, and more generally by the public. Public discourse often describes online shitstorms as triggered by minute online activity, like uploading a seemingly innocuous photograph or statement, and that social backlash is inevitable. Those who contribute to the shaming and other harms make up an unforgiving media assemblage. At other moments it identifies parts of this assemblage – like a specific commenter – as responsible for these outcomes. We can acknowledge that many actors play a role in contributing to online mobilisations in general. On the other hand, pinpointing a person, or a category of persons (e.g. 'trolls') seems to absolve all others of responsibility for harmful outcomes. A tabloid can blame online mobs for the harm that come to targets, even if they also play a role in cultivating this abuse. We can speculate that this reflects a formal versus informal distinction. The 'nobody is responsible' perspective seems to reflect a formal side of social sanction:

it is *sui generis* as a social process, with targets and participants both downstream from this decision to sanction. Punishment is inevitable not only as a part of a functional community, but also as a near-transcendent sense of justice and accountability. In contrast, 'everyone plays a role' seems to reflect an informal side: as actors who shape mediated shaming, we constantly exercise discretion in the severity of our reactions. Readers should pay attention to the role that dispersed actors play in cases of mediated denunciation, while conceding that most people will experience the mediated social sanction that they encounter – as targets, witnesses or eager participants – as a seemingly immutable force.

Second, we identify a tension between justice and entertainment as confluent motives in mediated shaming. The court of public opinion – manifest as online shitstorms – serves a vital role in people's lives when seeking justice. Within it, we recognise a gamut of criminological functions, from punishment to protection to socialisation (cf. Garland, 1993). Yet it also functions as a form of entertainment. This is not just to amuse audiences, but to engage them, which in turn compels people to cause more harm through vitriolic content. It may feel inevitable that the partial and proportionate nature of justice-seeking and restitution will be distorted or even subverted by media engagement. For this reason, any form of meaningful social justice processes or public safety reassurance should remain distinct and untampered from entertainment meant to generate a marketable audience for advertising revenue. Public deliberation and social justice should not have to be viral to be impactful. Yet this is an ideal that is quickly abandoned in an era when even public broadcasters are mindful of online metrics as a measure of success and see themselves moving towards a more clickbait style of reporting (Blanchett, 2021).

Third, and related to the justice/entertainment confluence, we must also reckon with mediated shaming calling upon people both as civilians and as an audience. People participate in scrutiny, shaming and denunciation because they are invested in local terrains, which may reflect both their capital and privilege, and also their vulnerability when facing job loss or embodied harm. Yet these practices are not only performed through screens – a mundane detail these days – but by producing content that somehow has a measurable impact on platforms. The practice of citizenship goes beyond local boundaries and is embedded in media business models. If these platforms are designed to cultivate outrage, civilian and citizen practices risk being distorted towards media-friendly forms of revelation and scandal.

Based on these tensions, we can question what kind of subjectivity is being created (cf. Koskela, 2004). In reflecting on media practice more generally, people identify a "main character syndrome,"[6] in which people centre and privilege their own agency and experiences over others. We can build on this admittedly crude pop-psychology characterisation through media practices considered in this book. Main characters engage digitally mediated social networks, seeing themselves as the most important and central node. And their interactions with a broader social network – whether an intimate peer group or a digital platform with over a billion users – involve observing and reporting on those they encounter digitally or in person. Not all who participate in mediated shaming have main character syndrome, but we can speculate that main characters are especially compelled to author content denouncing others, to draw an easy audience.[7] Thus, the main cameraperson, or main reporter syndrome is an equally valid phenomenon to study. We can begin to conceptualise it as a mediated form of bearing witness (hence the civil society/justice-seeking functionality) that is motivated and shaped by a disciplined and routinised publishing of content to cultivate social clout (hence the audience/entertainment dimensions). In studying grievance media content creators we can begin to unpack the cultural and ideological assembly of the 'main cameraperson syndrome,' through direct appeals as well as indirect shaping of surveillant imaginaries through portrayals of those who record and upload content in fictional media and non-fictional current affairs reporting.

Grievance media studies as an unfinished project

In this book we attempt to provide a global and experiential perspective of mediated shaming. In doing so, we draw on conversations with relevant people and close readings of relevant texts and discourses, rather than a quantitative overview of activities relating to interpersonal grievance in the media. Such an overview may be difficult for researchers to access, especially as platforms like Reddit and Twitter take a more miserly approach to granting access to platform data.[8] Moreover, such a quantitative approach may need to follow more rigid assumptions about guiding concepts, namely what 'counts' as mediated shaming, and what may fit as similar yet distinct practices like bullying, corporate-shaming or activism. We believe more work needs to be done to trouble these distinctions, to develop a more robust and nuanced understanding of how these conceptual boundaries are asserted by those engaging in shaming, those being shamed and those producing commentary on shaming for public engagement. Likewise, broader understandings of public opinion as a guiding concept provide important directions for further study. Here we can consider the role of so-called opinion leaders (Weimann, 1991) in stoking as well as downplaying cases of mediated denunciation. Moreover, we may find such opinion leaders in localised communities but also as prominent media figures, as employed or otherwise embedded within media platforms and even occupying official roles within a state regime.

Our account of mediated shaming reflects diverse perspectives, while omitting others. These decisions reflect the constraints of a compact manuscript, but also our own capabilities and limitations as researchers. Despite our cultural and linguistic fluency with the contexts studied, we are often outsiders to the communities we observe and write about. As a result, we are not able to provide a first-hand understanding of the cultural backdrop that stages any given public denunciation. We offer a global and more abstract account, while subsequent research can concentrate on specific cultural and institutional settings. Researchers can narrow their scope to specific kinds of offences. In addition to expanding a scholarship focus on denunciation against child sexual abuse as well as racist and sexist offences, we will also benefit from studies looking at the sensemaking and justification of mediated shaming against other types of offences, especially those that may otherwise not receive as much attention in public discourse. Researchers and those living in these mediated conditions can identify practices users employ to protect themselves and others against disproportionate harm, whether in hyperlocal neighbourhood clusterings, hobbyist communities or enthusiastic fandoms.

In terms of institutions, mediated shaming is a prominent yet understudied occurrence in the service and cultural sectors. Consider "*service de marde*" [shit service] groups that report on poor quality food from restaurants, which inescapably reflects on the people producing and delivering these meals.[9] Even when employees are not named or photographed, details included in written posts can help identify them to their employers and a general public. Likewise, employees of public service providers also face heightened scrutiny through digital media, often under a banner of 'wasting tax dollars.' In these cases, we can speculate that employer-employee relations are reconfigured through new forms of external oversight and intervention. More cynically, we may suspect that employers will use the guise of public accountability to enforce more demanding work conditions, along with austerity in pay and benefits. Here we can make sense of prominent visibility by way of two strands of professional literature. First, job market advice for individuals seeking to protect their reputation, or at least limit the fallout in cases of public shaming.[10] This is especially salient for those seeking work that involves being visible to a broader public. Second, we can rely on human resource management[11] and public relations[12] guidelines to understand how corporations are taught to handle employees becoming a liability via digital media shaming. Both researchers and job candidates themselves should be attentive to conditions to becoming public-facing, including dispersed and diverse understandings of how publicly available reputational data is generated across settings, as well as the kinds of mediated scrutiny practices that accompany these. We can examine how the self-presentation of job candidates on LinkedIn may resemble the trajectory of a prominent influencer struggling with an engagement economy on platforms like TikTok and YouTube. We can hypothesise that there is no rigid barrier between either set of conditions and practices, such that a similar vocabulary and imagery could be used to make sense of the struggle to become more prominent on any of these platforms.

There are also media actors who should receive more attention in research and popular accounts of mediated denunciation. When talking about engagement economies, we need to account for the role of advertisers in financing and benefiting from these forms of engagement. Advertisers may face backlash if their brands are directly and visibly linked to harmful witch hunts. But these witch hunts may keep users dwelling on platforms like Facebook and Reddit in a more general sense, and thus made available to advertisers for "facilitating commercial transactions" (Ørmen & Gregersen, 2023, p. 226). Likewise, our understanding of surveillant imaginaries can be enhanced by considering the role popular fiction plays in shaping shared understandings of appropriate conduct online. This is especially apparent when speculative fiction acknowledges and plays with the link between the fictional worlds they portray and the real digital media conditions we live in. The dystopian television series *Black Mirror* not only released episodes like *Hated in the Nation* and *Nosedive* that address the digitisation of social scoring and sanction, but also promoted the latter episode by releasing a "tongue-in-cheek" yet fully functional app for audiences to rate their peers.[13] These efforts can be understood in relation to previous platforms where people are rated, like Peeple and the public backlash its CEO met, prompting her to also "set the record straight" on *Dr. Phil.*[14] Returning to our opening example of BitClout, the potential to financially speculate on people's public standing is a troubling development that would not be out of place in a work of speculative fiction. At the time of writing, BitClout appears to be supplanted by friend.tec h, the most recent iteration of this model which is also being framed in the press as part of a passing trend.[15] We can analyse the kinds of reputational practices people would perform to either boost or devalue the 'stock' of a targeted individual, and in particular the role that mediated visibility would play in enabling these practices.

Even if the speculative stock model is fleeting, concerned individuals can continue to engage in review bombing to harm targeted individuals by way of products and services connected to them. We can expect that abuse of rating platforms – and attempts by platforms to rehabilitate their functionality and reputation – will remain a struggle. Those engaged in shaming will find new ways to make their weaponised reviews seem like legitimate grievances about the service being offered by the target, while platforms may invest in novel ways to detect and prevent reviews by those deemed 'illegitimate.' It may also be the case that platforms that solicit reviews embrace the toxic and weaponised nature of the content they circulate.

Closing words

Any case of mediated shaming may be contested as illegitimate. Audiences frequently question the agendas and biases of those who use mediated visibility to denounce others. It is easy to appraise those in the court of public opinion as acting in bad faith. This is in part due to political polarisation, as left/right, red-state/blue-state or 'woke'/'based' distinctions necessitate a binary sense of justice, and of condoning and condemning. In a polarised political and media landscape, any social developments can be readily mapped onto one side of prominent cultural fault-lines. Yet there remains the possibility of a non-partisan pushback against not only forms of personal scrutiny that we recognise as excessive and abusive, but also forms of disproportionate public shaming in cases where someone is denounced. Non-partisan terms of excessive shaming will be difficult to determine in highly contested domains, such as denunciation against classroom 'indoctrination.' We wonder if a community can come to an agreement about how to use digital media to punish bad parking. So-called 'petty' offences can also reflect cultural fault-lines, yet they seem like a more manageable starting point to create firm and situated guidelines for digitally mediated social sanction. Media audiences appear capable of transcending polarisation when agreeing that a targeted individual is abhorrent, whether that is an influencer on holiday during lockdown, or a stranger gratuitously harming animals. A possible next step is to identify cases that a broader populace can acknowledge as generating a disproportionate backlash, using these as an opportunity to revisit and renegotiate norms of acceptable behaviour on digital platforms – and when using mobile devices in face-to-face settings – in order to prevent such cases from happening again.

In thinking thusly, we can begin to envision and work towards a court of public opinion that is not entangled in media exploitation of reputation, yet remains a prominent, localised and responsive tool for social justice. The next public health crisis that augments social scrutiny may be compounded by war and climate disasters, alongside fuel and food shortages, but also by wide-scale adoption of AI to further disrupt relations with others. While current media conditions are troubling, anybody concerned or at least fascinated by mediated shaming should anticipate how these conditions may evolve in new states of exception, especially if these facilitate reputational harm, and subsequently other harms like denial of critical support.

Notes

1 https://docs.bitclout.com/
2 https://decrypt.co/62770/inside-bitclout-dystopian-social-network-big-investors-vocal-critics
3 https://www.coindesk.com/tech/2021/03/22/what-is-bitclout-the-social-media-experiment-sparking-controversy-on-twitter/
4 https://www.thewrap.com/cinnamon-toast-crunch-guy-jensen-karp-abuse-allegations/
5 https://www.advisoryexcellence.com/keyboard-warriors-say-things-online-but-not-in-person/
6 https://www.psychologytoday.com/us/blog/digital-world-real-world/202106/the-trouble-main-character-syndrome
7 Consider the frequency of such cases on the following subreddit: https://www.reddit.com/r/ImTheMainCharacter/

8 https://www.forbes.com/sites/antoniopequenoiv/2023/06/13/reddit-stands-by-controversial-api-changes-as-subreddit-protest-continues/; https://www.wired.com/story/twitter-data-api-prices-out-nearly-everyone/
9 https://www.lesacdechips.com/2023/08/22/un-employe-de-burger-king-refuse-de-mettre-des-oignons-dans-un-whopper-et-ca-fait-reagir-sur-la-page-spotted-service-de-marde
10 https://www.huffpost.com/entry/cost-of-online-shaming-to-your-career-and-love-life_b_5a05dc4fe4b0ee8ec36940fb
11 https://www.shrm.org/mena/executive-network/insights/avoiding-social-media-anarchy-8-tips-ceos
12 https://www.prnewsonline.com/yes-justine-sacco-really-said-that-on-twitter/
13 https://www.wired.co.uk/article/rate-me-nosedive-black-mirror-netflix
14 https://www.cbc.ca/news/canada/calgary/peeple-founder-to-appear-on-dr-phil-show-1.3268616
15 https://cointelegraph.com/news/friendtech-social-media-app-how-long-will-it-last

References

Abrahams, R. (1998). *Vigilant citizens: vigilantism and the state*. Polity.

Blanchett, N. (2021). Quantifying quality: Negotiating audience participation and the value of a digital story at NRK. *Journalism Practice*, *15*(10), 1541–1561. https://doi.org/10.1080/17512786.2020.1791231

Couldry, N. (2002). *Media rituals: A critical approach*. Routledge. https://doi.org/10.4324/9780203986608

Garfinkel, H. (1956). Conditions of successful degradation ceremonies. *American Journal of Sociology*, *61*(5), 420–424. https://doi.org/10.1086/221800

Garland, D. (1993). *Punishment and modern society: A study in social theory*. University of Chicago Press. https://doi.org/10.7208/chicago/9780226922508.001.0001

Gill, R. (2023). *Perfect: Feeling judged on social media*. John Wiley & Sons. https://doi.org/10.1080/09589236.2024.2320974

Gray, J. (2005). Antifandom and the moral text: Television without pity and textual dislike. *American Behavioral Scientist*, *48*(7), 840–858. https://doi.org/10.1177/0002764204273171

Koskela, H. (2004). Webcams, TV shows and mobile phones: Empowering exhibitionism. *Surveillance & Society*, *2*(2/3), 199–215. https://doi.org/10.24908/ss.v2i2/3.3374

Ørmen, J., & Gregersen, A. (2023). Towards the engagement economy: Interconnected processes of commodification on YouTube. *Media, Culture & Society*, *45*(2), 225–245. https://doi.org/10.1177/01634437221111951

Thompson, J. B. (2005). The new visibility. *Theory, Culture & Society*, *22*(6), 31–51. https://doi.org/10.1177/0263276405059413

Vallas, S. P., & Christin, A. (2018). Work and identity in an era of precarious employment: How workers respond to “personal branding” discourse. *Work and Occupations*, *45*(1), 3–37. https://doi.org/10.1177/0730888417735662

Wade, M. (2022). ‘The giving layer of the internet’: A critical history of GoFundMe’s reputation management, platform governance, and communication strategies in capturing peer-to-peer and charitable giving markets.*Journal of Philanthropy and Marketing*, *28*(4), 1–18. https://doi.org/10.1002/nvsm.1777

Weimann, G. (1991). The influentials: Back to the concept of opinion leaders?. *Public Opinion Quarterly*, *55*(2), 267–279. https://doi.org/10.1086/269257

Index

For Product Safety Concerns and Information please contact our EU representative GPSR@taylorandfrancis.com
Taylor & Francis Verlag GmbH, Kaufingerstraße 24, 80331 München, Germany

www.ingramcontent.com/pod-product-compliance
Lightning Source LLC
Chambersburg PA
CBHW061753270326
41928CB00011B/2484